This Book is Dedicated to the City of Springfield,
Its Newspapers,
And the Many Hundreds of People
Who Have Given of Their Time, Fortunes, and Energy
To Bring the Gillioz "Theatre Beautiful"
Back to Life.

Beggar: Lady, could you give me a quarter to get where my family is?
Lady: Certainly, my poor man, here's a quarter. Where is your family?
Beggar: At the movies....

THE GILLIOZ "THEATRE BEAUTIFUL":
Remembering Springfield's Theatre History, 1926-2006

An Illustrated History
Marking the Gala Reopening of the Gillioz Theatre
in Springfield, Missouri, October 2006

Edited by James S. Baumlin
Missouri State University

Preface by the Hon. Roy Blunt
Southwest Missouri Congressman

Moon City Press
Springfield, Missouri

First published in the United States in 2006 by Moon City Press.
Copyright © 2006 Moon City Press

ISBN: 0-913785-05-9

Library of Congress Control Number: 2006933765

Printed in the United States

The Gillioz "Theatre Beautiful" is a cooperative project of the
following academic and community partners:
The Springfield Landmarks Preservation Trust
The Missouri State University College of Arts and Letters
The Missouri State University Department of English
The Missouri State University Department of Art and Design
The Special Collections and Archives of Missouri State University
The Ozarks Studies Institute of Missouri State University
The History Museum for Springfield-Greene County
The Writers Hall of Fame® of America
Lawrence Photo and Video

Designed by Eric Pervukhin

Contents

Preface

Congressman Roy Blunt
Missouri 7th District

The history of the Gillioz "Theatre Beautiful" reflects that of the city of Springfield, Missouri. Some of the most important chapters in their joint history are the visits by Ronald Reagan, first as Hollywood actor, then as America's 40th President. On June 7, 2002, the Gillioz marked the 50th anniversary of Reagan's movie, *The Winning Team*, which held its world premiere at the theater. I was privileged to be part of this celebration. On that same day, it was my honor to preside over the dedication of the Ronald and Nancy Reagan Center, which boasts the restored Gillioz Theatre as its crown jewel. It is now my pleasure to recommend this illustrated history to readers interested in theater, in Springfield and in President Reagan.

The Gillioz "Theatre Beautiful": Remembering Springfield's Theatre History, 1926-2006 traces the venue's (and the city's) rich history through the Roaring Twenties, the Great Depression, the Second World War, the Cold War, the Sixties and the Seventies, recounting the many live acts and films that graced the theater's stage and screen. The book's authors explore the cultural and economic impact that theatrical entertainment has had on Springfield and the Ozarks. The authors demonstrate how this entertainment helped shape the city's corporate identity. This book is more than the story of a downtown theater's birth, growth, decline, closing, and restoration; it is also a comprehensive social history of modern Springfield. While written for a popular audience, this book is perhaps the most detailed study published to date on the subject of downtown Springfield.

We have reason to be proud of The Gillioz Theatre's restoration and reopening. I invite all of Springfield and Southwest Missouri to join me in this celebration.

The Gillioz "Theatre Beautiful": Celebrating Springfield's Theatre History, 1926-2006 is the first fruit of ENCORE 2006, an ongoing collaboration between the Missouri State University's College of Arts and Letters and the Gillioz Theatre Board of Directors. Featuring a series of public events scheduled for October, 2006, ENCORE 2006 commemorates the eightieth anniversary and gala reopening of the Gillioz. ENCORE 2006 will be the first of many such events held annually at the Gillioz, which will bring University faculty, students, and community partners together in celebration of the arts and letters. ENCORE 2006 demonstrates the College's commitment to the Missouri State University's mission in public affairs, taking students out of the classroom and into the larger community, where their artistic talents and scholarly expertise can best be displayed and utilized.

ENCORE 2006 began as an informal conversation between Wade Thompson, Acting Head of the Theatre and Dance Department, and Tom Croley, a member of the Gillioz Theatre Board. Their conversation led to formal discussions between Nancy Brown Dornan, President of the Gillioz Theatre Board, Dr. Gloria Galanes, Dean, and Marie Murphree, Director of Development, College of Arts and Letters. In September, 2005, faculty representatives from the College's seven departments—Art and Design; Communication; English; Media, Journalism, and Film; Modern and Classical Languages; Music; and Theatre and Dance—met with Dornan to explore collaborations between the College and the Gillioz. In January, 2006, ENCORE 2006 was officially launched: led by Dr. Carol Anne Costabile-Heming, Associate Dean, each department made plans to participate in a month-long series of public exhibitions, readings, film showings and live performances.

ENCORE 2006 will include a display of artwork by students and faculty in Art and Design. An original live-variety show (written and produced for the Gillioz reopening) will showcase the Music Department's Opera Workshop, the Pride Marching Band, and other student musicians, dancers, and actors. ENCORE 2006 will also feature a review of American musical theater. Media, Journalism, and Film will offer an installment of its regular MJF Film Series, as well as showings of student video productions. The English Department will present one of its regular Moon City readings. And the Communication Department will host a student speech competition. In previous years, such events would have taken place on the Missouri State University campus; they would represent the regular classroom and studio work of students and faculty during a typical fall semester. With ENCORE 2006, these events will take place at the Gillioz Theatre in downtown Springfield.

ENCORE 2006 will culminate in an evening black-tie gala and an afternoon family gala featuring one of the University's top jazz bands and a concert performance of George Gershwin's

Rhapsody in Blue. Area arts groups will join students and faculty in several of these events. Groups participating in Encore 2006 include the Actors Theatre of Missouri, the Boys Choir of Springfield, the Missouri Film Alliance, the Ozark Showcase of Sweet Adelines, the Springfield Mid-America Singers, Moonlight Revue, the Springfield Parks and Recreation Board, the Springfield Regional Opera, and the Skinny Improv.

Encore 2006 expands the Missouri State University's community partnerships and its contributions to Springfield's downtown literary and artistic culture. In addition to this present book (a joint project of the Departments of English and Art and Design), a documentary video will be produced by the Department of Media, Journalism, and Film; this video will highlight the history of the Gillioz Theatre and document the planning, University-community collaborations, and events surrounding Encore 2006. For its part, the Gillioz Theatre Board will bury a twenty-five year time capsule to commemorate the reopening. The College of Arts and Letters and the Gillioz Theatre Board look forward to an Encore 2007, an Encore 2008, and so on through Encore 2031, when the time capsule will be opened and studied by a new generation of students, faculty, and community partners.

Researched and composed by students and their teacher in a graduate-level English seminar, *The Gillioz "Theatre Beautiful"* has been written by scholars for a popular audience. Its authors apologize for any residual pedantry left over in a book whose primary aim is to please. A theater's variety-vaudeville acts and "photoplays" ran continuously throughout the day. It hardly mattered when audiences arrived; sooner or later, the show cycled back to the beginning. And the audience was free to stay as long as it liked. The theater was never forcibly emptied, as it is with today's multiplex-cinematic cattle drives. So with this book: a reader may pick and choose her entry points, staying in any chapter only so long as she wishes. For all their aiming to please, chapter three and the coda remain mighty stuffy. If the reader doesn't care all that much about the social history of Springfield and vaudeville, she can leave these or other sections and enter again elsewhere; the scene changes quickly enough.

To streamline the narrative, the book's scholarly apparatus has been reduced to quoted sources. Please note the following abbreviations, which we use throughout:

DD   Harris Dark and Phyllis Dark, *Springfield of the Ozarks: An Illustrated History* (1981).

G   Wayne Glenn, *The Ozarks' Greatest Hits: A Photo History of Music in the Ozarks* (2005).

LL   Robert S. Lynd and Helen Merrell Lynd, *Middletown: A Study of American Culture* (1929).

M   Albert F. McLean, *American Vaudeville as Ritual* (1965).

R   Milton D. Rafferty, *The Ozarks: Land and Life* (2001).

S   Anthony Slide (ed.), *Selected Vaudeville Criticism* (1988).

For a complete list of sources (including interviews), readers may consult an expanded typescript of this text, which is available in the Special Collections and Archives of Missouri State University.

The internet has revolutionized research, and much of our information regarding Springfield history, theater history, and film history comes from the web: the *All Movie Guide* (for reviews), the *American Film Institute* (for release dates), *Cinema Treasures* (for house openings and closings), *Gillioz.org* (for the theater restoration), *NewspaperArchive.com* (for vaudeville), and *Richgros.com* (for local history) are sites that we visited time and again.

Though most web information must be taken with salt, these sites have offered reliable starting points for our research.

Of course the city's newspapers remain the most important, most authoritative source for our broad subject. Through early decades of the Twentieth Century, Springfield was served by two papers: the *Daily News* (named the *Republican* prior to 1927) and the *Leader* (the one-time *Democrat*). In 1929, H. S. Jewell (owner of the Jefferson Theater, later renamed the Jewell) began publishing an afternoon and Sunday paper, the *Springfield Press*. Pressured by the Depression economy, the latter two merged in 1933, forming the *Leader and Press*. In 1985 the *Daily News* and *Leader and Press* merged to form today's *Springfield News-Leader*. Readers might keep this evolution of newspaper titles in mind.

≈ ≈

We have many individuals to thank, as many contributed: Murray Bishoff of the *Monett Times,* Dr. Byrne Blackwood, Nancy Brown Dornan, Bob Bryant, Dr. Carol Anne Costabile-Heming, Dr. Tom Dicke, Gary Ellison, Mary Sue Fox, Sam Freeman, Melodie Harrington, Wayne Glenn, Dr. Rachel Gholson, Sharol Higgins Neely of the Springfield-Greene County Library District, Darrin J. Rodgers of the Flower Pentecostal Heritage Center, John E. Sellars, Mark Shipley of Lawrence Photo and Video, Rachel Wright, and Dr. Pearl Yeadon-Erny. Missouri State University archivist David Richards and his staff—Anne M. Baker, Tracie Gieselman-Holthaus, Shannon Western, and Anita Roberts—remained fiercely loyal to this project. Joan Hampton-Porter yielded to us the riches of the History Museum for Springfield-Greene County. Without the expertise, encouragement, and help of these many, our project could never have come to fruition.

Finally, this book stands upon the shoulders of those local giants who wrote before us: Shanna Boyle and Julie March, Skip Curtis, Harris Dark and Phyllis Dark, Wayne Glenn, Richard Grosenbaugh, Sony Hocklander, Mike O'Brien, Reta Spears-Stewart, Tracey Rainey, Bil Tatum, and Jim Wunderle.

"You can take your choice. Either do as I tell you or leave."

Mr. Perdue and his son Clint stood facing each other. Mr. Perdue was an old lawyer. People called him "set." He knew it, and as the seriousness of the controversy between himself and his oldest boy unfolded before his keen and penetrating mind he thought of himself half whimsically as, "Sixty and set." ...

Clint was twenty years old and had always obeyed his father. But the same setness that was in the older man was also in the boy, possibly in a slightly intensified degree. He had asked his father several times to be allowed to attend the movies, but had been refused....

This morning he had said to his father, "I'm going to take Amy to the movies tonight, Dad."

Mr. Perdue turned sharply when he heard this extraordinary statement, and when he looked into the steady, level eyes of his son, ... he knew that the tug of war had come at last....

"I've told you times-a-plenty that boys and girls can learn devilment enough without going to take a term in a school of devilry. If you go, you may pack your duds and leave." ...

"I'm going, Dad," he said. His voice was husky and weak, but his eyes did not fail....

"Call at the bank as you go by, if you leave. I'll tell Chiswell to let you have a hundred dollars. Don't write me until you are ready to come back and do right. The old place will be waiting for you whenever you want to return, but there must be obedience in my home. Goodbye, Clint." ...

—"Seeing Stars," by Rajoma. Published in the March 11, 1928 *Christ's Ambassadors: A Paper for the Young People* by the Gospel Publishing House of the Assemblies of God, Springfield, Missouri.

1. October 11, 1926: The Opening

Greetings:

In the opening of the Gillioz Theatre a splendid contribution is made to the amusement resources of the community. This is the largest, finest and most modern, exclusive motion picture theater in Southwest Missouri. The management has spared neither effort nor expense in making it worthy in every way of the intelligent and exacting public, which it has been built to serve.

This superb structure lends a new dignity and a new importance to the City of Springfield, and we pledge ourselves that the entertainment given on the screen will be worthy of the house and its patrons, and representative of the highest ideals in pictorial drama.

The Gillioz Theatre has been built on the same scale as those in leading amusement centers. The mission of a theater is to entertain, and this can now be done as efficiently as in the larger cities. On this occasion, your initial visit, we bid you each and all a sincere and hearty welcome.

—*Gillioz Souvenir Book*,
October 11, 1926

"A Beautiful Theatre for Springfield."

On Sunday morning, October 10—the day before the theater's opening—the city's two rival newspapers overflowed with Gillioz articles and advertisements, making it difficult to tell one from the other. (See figure: "A Beautiful Theatre for Springfield.") "M. E. Gillioz is Rightfully Proud of His New Theater," announced one headline. The man (who pronounced his name *Gilloyz*) placed his own full-page ad, declaring his theater "A new high mark in architectural beauty." "Courtesy to be Main Policy at the New Gillioz," proclaimed another headline. Courtesy, indeed: the theater promised no less than "Fairyland." (See figure: "Wonderland Gillioz.") As the management's own bold front-page ad declared,

Tomorrow, [in] only 24 hours, the Gillioz opens and the crowds and throngs of Springfieldians and visitors will come from everywhere to attend the Greatest Event Ever Held in Springfield. Make no appointment, you must be present at this tremendous opening. You'll behold: Fairyland—at the greatest show place in Springfield. It's ready for you and it's yours. It's waiting for you—gorgeous, vivid, awe inspiring, dazzling, sweeping, amazing, bewildering!

The language is half Hollywood, half circus-huckstering. Still, to those Springfieldians lucky enough to attend its gala opening, the Gillioz likely seemed "the greatest show place" in town. And the theater's management looked for more than local fame. As yet another ad declared, "No expense has been spared to give the music loving public of Springfield those same marvelous musical treats now enjoyed by audiences that throng the great theaters in New York, Chicago, St. Louis and hundreds of other cities coast to coast." (See insert: Theatre or Theater?)

By comparing itself to "the great theaters in New

"Wonderland Gillioz."

the City of Springfield." A town that could boast such a theater was no mere town: it could declare itself a "City," one whose "music loving public" shared the same interests, and now the same facilities, as "other cities coast to coast." Though "Heart of the Ozarks," Springfield could also (and quite legitimately) claim rough equality and connection with these "hundreds of other cities." The Frisco Railroad and Route 66 would see to this. And as citizens of a modern, affluent, progressive nation, Springfieldians deserved "the same marvelous musical treats" as Californians and New Yorkers.

The Gillioz made good on its claims, as "no expense" had been spared, whether in the theater's amenities, in its booking of live acts, or in the latest film technologies. As proof, the opening night's playbill featured the Swiss Song Birds, a vaudeville act bringing its own scenery and special lighting all the way from Grumman's Million Dollar Theater in Los Angeles. From the East Coast came a newsreel of the sixth game of the 1926 World Series, featuring the St. Louis Cardinals against the New York Yankees. Filmed in Yankee Stadium on Saturday, October 9—a mere two days before the gala opening—the reel was flown into Springfield for the first show. (See figure:"Come if You Have to Fly.") The first night's features reached literally from coast to coast.

The theater doors opened at 6:00 p.m. on October 11, with performances at 7:00 p.m. and 9:00 p.m. Arriving well ahead of time, would-be patrons waited in two lines, one stretching westward on St. Louis Street to the Public Square, the other stretching eastward to Jefferson Avenue where it turned north, snaking its way onto Olive Street. The next morning's *Springfield Leader* described "a crowd big enough to fill the theater three

York, Chicago, St. Louis" (that is, to New York's Palladium, Chicago's Palace, and St. Louis's Orpheum) the Gillioz asserted its place—and, by extension, Springfield's place—on the national scene. No longer would Springfield seem "merely" regional, largely isolated and nationally insignificant, lying at the margins (though geographically in the center) of America's increasingly urban interests and entertainments. As the *Gillioz Souvenir Book* asserted on its opening page, "This superb structure lends a new dignity and a new importance to

"Come if You Have to Fly."

Theatre or Theater? While newspaper ads consistently refer to the Gillioz "Theatre Beautiful," following British usage, the **Souvenir Book** is offered "Compliments of the Gillioz Theater," following American usage. **Which is correct?** Perhaps the mixed spelling reflects Springfield's own "dual class" citizenry. "Theatre Beautiful" suggests elegance, affluence, opulence—a European-aristocratic mythology, to which American white-collar audiences pretended and blue-collar audiences aspired. Albert F. McLean notes the appeal such grand palaces as the Gillioz made to America's ascendant "mercantile middle class" (M41), "with its steadily increasing affluence, its appetite for consumer goods, its ambitions for its children, and its awed envy of the wealthy and socially prominent" (M42). Several of the more formal Gillioz advertisements play to this tails-and-top-hat fantasy. Yet other ads, clearly lower in the brow, caricature the tuxedoed Gillioz patron, stressing action, adventure, melodrama, comedy, fun—an escape and refreshment following the long day's labor. On October 11, 1926 some small portion of Springfield's citizens might don tuxes; the rest put on their Sunday best. Both classes would meet and mingle in the Gillioz lobbies, the "Theatre Beautiful" serving as the community's latest, greatest social leveller.

So, we'll write officially of the Gillioz "Theatre Beautiful," deferring in this case to British usage. Otherwise, in good-old American English, we'll write of the Springfield theatergoer, theater architecture and technology, and the theater industry generally.

Gillioz on Opening Night.

or four times, and so eager was the multitude to witness the premier [that] a police line had to be formed at the entrance. It was a mad scramble for tickets and the house was rapidly filled." As the *Leader* headline declared, "Magnificent New Playhouse Turned Away Thousands Who Awaited Hours to Witness Premier Performance." (See figure: Gillioz on Opening Night.)

Admission was forty cents for adults, ten cents for children. Yet the price of admission covered more than vaudeville, news reels, and a feature film: it covered admission to the new theater itself. Sandwiched

Gillioz Marquee and Façade.

between the elegant Netter's Department Store and a plain Western Union storefront, the theater's St. Louis Street façade and entrance made an impressive sight, with its Hollywood-inspired Spanish-Mediterranean architecture, colorful terra-cotta facing and three-sided, canopied marquee. (See figure: Gillioz Marquee and Façade.) Incandescent lighting surrounded the art-deco marquee and vertical sign. Inset in the terra-cotta tile work above the marquee stood an arched stained-glass window: illuminated from within, it emblazoned the builder's signature "G." Sheltered within the recessed entrance bay, a

Gillioz Entrance Bay.

small box office stood islanded on the tile and terrazzo sidewalk. (See figure: Gillioz Entrance Bay.)

Through the entrance bay three sets of leaded-glass French double-doors opened into the narrow outer lobby, some sixty foot long by twenty foot wide. Just beyond the French doors a variable feast of sights, sounds, and scents awaited those lucky Springfieldians who had gotten tickets. Huge banks of flowers—sent to the management from all parts of the country—adorned both sides of the long, high-ceilinged, finely-decorated hallway, hiding much of the ground floor's ornamentation; likely they accented the turquoise, bronze, and gold interior. Their fragrance competed with the aroma of freshly-

Gillioz Outer Lobby.

Gillioz Orchestra Foyer.

popped, buttered popcorn and the smell of clean, new carpeting. Patrons would have found it a pleasant enough standing room, had they the patience for waiting. (See figure: Gillioz Outer Lobby.) Of course, smoking was allowed.

At the end of the long outer lobby another three sets of doors opened into a more ornate inner lobby. Here patrons trod delicately upon plush maroon carpeting (a luxury at the time). From this comfortable waiting room, a carpeted staircase led up to the mezzanine. Beneath the staircase a concession booth—tiny by today's standards—was tucked away. Perfect for people-watching, the mezzanine balcony overlooked the long outer foyer, while the mezzanine rotunda looked down upon the first floor inner lobby. Matching wrought-iron balustrades ran along the staircase, balcony, and rotunda. (See figure: Gillioz Mezzanine Rotunda.) The scene would have delighted, as mezzanine patrons people-watched over the balustrades, gazing down upon patrons entering below. The mezzanine, too, overflowed with flowers.

Beyond the first floor's inner lobby (just past the concession booth) patrons entered yet another anteroom, the orchestra foyer. Running the width of the house, this lavishly-decorated hallway separated the lobby's noisy waiting crowds from audiences inside. The orchestra foyer sported alcoves hung with draperies of heavy damasks, velours, and satins. (See figure: Gillioz Orchestra Foyer.) From the mezzanine lobby, a second set of stairs led up to the balcony foyer, which held offices and the theater's rest rooms. Tiny and totally inadequate by today's standards, the men's room contained one stall and two urinals, the ladies' room three stalls, all to serve a capacity crowd of 1,120.

Architecturally the best came last, as the Spanish-inspired red, blue, and gold-gilt auditorium was meant to awe. The proscenium arch surrounding the stage dazzled with its riot of floral moldings and medallions. (See figure: Gillioz Stage.) Flanking the shallow proscenium were pairs of gilt arcades with double arches and plaster grilles, behind which stood the theater's organ pipes.

Gillioz Mezzanine Rotunda.

Gillioz Stage.

(Actually the pipes occupied the west arcade only. If a little money had been saved by this means, the patrons needn't be told.) Separated by decorative columns, each arcade overlooked a balconet whose apron sported plaster urns, garlands, and winged cherubs. (See figure: Gillioz East Arcade.)

A decorative balustrade ran along the balcony, which reached out over half the orchestra floor. The projection room sat nestling at the balcony's top. (See figure: Gillioz Balcony.) Frescoed in sunlight gold, the ceiling featured a large recessed oculus, a shallow dome whose center gave the appearance of an open eye (children squinting up might imagine the Almighty One staring down at them). All told, it was an impressive, imposing sight.

❧ ❧

Dressed in tuxedo-styled uniforms of dark gray with red lapels and white gloves, ten young men served as ushers, each moving with a grace bespeaking training and hours of practice. With utmost courtesy (as promised by the Gillioz management) these elegant, well-mannered ushers led guests to their seats, presenting each with a classy *Souvenir Book*. After securing their seats, patrons whiled away the time with more people-watching, admiring the architecture and leafing through the program. In attendance were representatives of Warner Brothers, Universal, Capitol, Fox, Metro, Paramount, Western Vaudeville Managers Association, and numerous booking agencies. Also present were special guests of the builder, M. E. Gillioz: thirty-seven dignitaries from Jefferson City, fifteen from his hometown of Monett, three from Willow Springs, two each from St. Louis and Nixa, and one each from Friestatt, Joplin, Ozark, Rolla, and Rosebud.

In its front-page article, the October 12 *Springfield Republican* described the ceremony: "The evening's program was opened by organist Glen Stambach, who played

Reginald Denny Sends His Regards. *In the early days of film, stars (rather, their managers) kept up the pretense and etiquette of the live stage: hence Denny's October 11 telegram declaring his pleasure in opening the theater. "Mr. Denny had planned to attend the opening," the* Leader *added, but "it was impossible for him to reach Springfield." Of equal interest is his second telegram, published in the next day's* Republican*: "That certainly was a reception Springfield gave my latest photoplay last night at the gala-opening of the Gillioz theater-beautiful. I want to express my sincere appreciation to you all and promise to give you even finer productions in the future". Denny writes as though he had been present himself, having taken bows to the applause. Yes, audiences would have applauded a fine film performance: such is the convention of live theater, which carried over to its film imitations.*

The romance of a Western Union Telegram, by the way, would have appealed doubly to Gillioz patrons, as the special nature of such messages announced both the importance of its news and the relative affluence of its sender—in this case, a famous British-born actor cabling from Hollywood. Fortunately, a Western Union Office stood just next door, to the theater's east. The pretense of telegramming audiences continued: see Clark Gable's cable advertisement announcing an upcoming film. (See figure: Gable Telegram.)

the National Anthem, and as the crowd rose to its feet, the front curtain of the stage was slowly raised and a floral horseshoe wreath bearing 'Success' across its center was bathed in a flood of light." Gillioz assistant manager Harry Wren then "took the stage and with a few words introduced Sam Wear, local attorney, who acted as master of ceremonies." (Wear later became Greene County Prosecuting Attorney and, under President Truman, U.S. District Attorney.) Wear, in turn, introduced City Attorney Dan Nee, who welcomed the new theater and its builder on the city's behalf. From his box seat, Mr. Gillioz bowed to "tumultuous applause." Attorney Perry Allen then presented the Gillioz manager, A. H. Bachman, with the horseshoe wreath. To conclude the dedication, Wear read several congratulatory telegrams "from various stars and theatrical men," including "Carl Laemmle, president of the Universal Film Corporation," and Reginald Denny, star of the evening's featured film. (See insert: Reginald Denny Sends His Regards.)

The audience was by now ready for the show, which the *Souvenir Book* touted as "one of the most interesting and well balanced theatrical performances ever witnessed in Springfield." First to perform was the "house band," Marvin Niles and his New Idea Orches-

Gillioz East Arcade.

Gillioz Balcony.

tra. A former Vaudeville musician on the Orpheum Circuit, Niles had made phonograph recordings and was familiar to Springfield audiences through Kansas City's WDAF Radio (which could be picked up most evenings in Springfield). The New Idea Orchestra kicked off the evening with the overture from Sigmund Romberg's 1924 operetta, *The Student Prince*. Some in the audience would have hummed along with its famous drinking song— "Drink! Drink! Drink! to eyes that are bright as stars when they're shining on me ... "— remembering a time before Prohibition when one could still drink, as well as sing, in public.

With the screen lowered over the hardwood stage, several film shorts followed: a Felix the Cat cartoon (silent, of course, and black-and-white), a reel of international news, and footage from the sixth game of the World Series—a game won by the Cardinals 10-2 behind their ace, Grover Cleveland Alexander, who scattered eight hits in the victory. The Redbirds would win the series the following day, with Alexander entering in relief. (Ironically, this very series and its pitching hero would feature in a second gala held on the Gillioz stage, one that would bring Mrs. Grover Cleveland Alexander to Springfield along with Ronald and Nancy Reagan: we refer to the world premiere of Ronald Reagan's 1952 film, *The Winning Team*, of which we'll have more to say later).

Glen Stambach, "singing organist" from Chicago, then offered an "Introduction of the Hope-Jones Organ," an instrument "capable of orchestrating the sounds of 300 different musical instruments," as the next day's *Leader* remarked. (See insert: The Gillioz Theatre's "Mighty Wurlitzer.") His finish, an audience sing-along to "Bye Bye Blackbird," used the latest technology of "throwing" or projecting the lyrics on screen, thus:

> Pack up all my care and woe,
> Here I go, singin' low:
> Bye bye blackbird.
> Where somebody waits for me
> Sugar's sweet, so is she:
> Bye bye blackbird.
> No one here can love or understand me.
> Oh, what hard luck stories they all hand me.
> Make my bed and light the light,
> I'll arrive late tonight:
> Blackbird, bye bye!

The evening's "three big time presentations" followed, beginning with a first-night only performance by the yodeling Swiss Song Birds. "Victor, Master Accordionist Extraordinary" next took the stage. Upon finishing his first performance he took his instrument out to the mezzanine lobby. Climbing on a chair by the rotunda, the Californian then

entertained the audience filing in for the 9:00 p.m. showing. Also booked for "Opening Night Only," the final headliners were Taylor and Martin, Kansas City's "Ukulele Songsters" and "WDAF Radio Stars." Like Marvin Niles, their live radio performances had made them familiar to Springfieldians. As the *Republican* noted, "each of these acts was greeted by much applause and proved highly popular with the large audience, many encores being demanded."

After the vaudeville came the feature film, *Take It From Me*, starring Reginald Denny. A seventy-minute silent "photoplay" comedy, it was filmed in the only option at that time: beautiful black and white. Denny plays a young man who has squandered his inheritance

The Gillioz Theatre's "Mighty Wurlitzer." To be precise, Glen Stambach played upon the Wurlitzer Hope-Jones Unit Orchestra Style D, Opus 1411. Shipped from the company's Tonawanda, New York plant on September 8, 1926, the Gillioz organ was the 1,411[th] of 2,238 instruments built by the Rudolph Wurlitzer Company between 1911 and 1943. One of the more popular theater organs (over 200 were built and shipped worldwide), Style D was a mid-sized instrument featuring two manuals, a curved bolster console, and six ranks of pipes plus extended notes for cathedral chimes, xylophone, and glockenspiel. Its percussion effects included bass drum, kettle drum, snare drum, cymbal, tambourine, castanets, tom tom, and sleigh bells. Style D sound effects included horse hoofs, bird, surf, auto horn, fire gong, steamboat whistle, siren, machine gun, and door bell. (The Electric Theatre, a downtown rival, owned the slightly more opulent Wurlitzer Style F, Opus 1306, featuring eight ranks of pipes.)

The "Mighty Wurlitzer," as such organs were fondly nicknamed, was a powerful, versatile, majestic instrument. For its "Introduction" Stambach would have pulled out the stops, emphasizing its lush musicality, its range of tones, timbres, and registers. He would likely have put the instrument through its theatrical paces as well, sampling its more realistic, more humorous sound effects—all to fill the silence of early film. More than competent musically, a theater organist had to be skilled at improvisation. For their major silent films the movie studios supplied musical scores; for most other films the musical accompaniment and sound effects were improvised "to fit the action on the screen" (Ellison, "Show Palaces" 27). Indeed the more creative organists manipulated the instrument's many pedals, keys, buttons, and pistons, inventing their own effects—a laugh, a cock crow, a pig's grunt, a lion's roar, an airplane.

Dismantled and sold in 1980, the original instrument is currently in private hands. If it is not returned to the theater, then an equally majestic replacement awaits refurbishing and installation. A Springfieldian and "award-winning photojournalist, who worked for *Life*, *Look* and *National Geographic* (Ellison, "Show Palaces" 27), Weldon King had a passion for theater organs, having played on the Gillioz Wurlitzer as a youth. To the delight of friends whom he regularly serenaded, King owned an eight-rank Robert Morton Theatre Organ—a "Wonder Morton," as this California-based Wurlitzer-rival was nicknamed—which he had installed in his home. Bequeathed to the Springfield Landmarks Preservation Trust, King's "Wonder Morton" now belongs to the Gillioz.

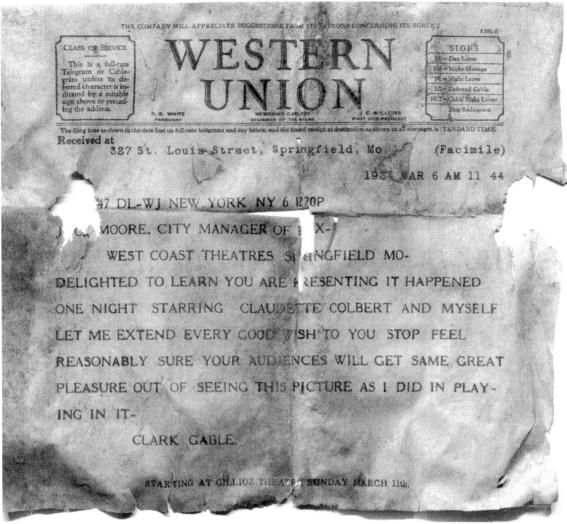

THE COMPANY WILL APPRECIATE SUGGESTIONS FROM ITS PATRONS CONCERNING ITS SERVICE

WESTERN UNION

Received at 327 St. Louis Street, Springfield, Mo.   (Facimile)

193_ MAR 6 AM 11 44

47 DL-WJ NEW YORK NY 6 220P

J. C. MOORE. CITY MANAGER OF FOX-

WEST COAST THEATRES SPRINGFIELD MO-

DELIGHTED TO LEARN YOU ARE PRESENTING IT HAPPENED
ONE NIGHT STARRING CLAUDETTE COLBERT AND MYSELF
LET ME EXTEND EVERY GOOD WISH TO YOU STOP FEEL
REASONABLY SURE YOUR AUDIENCES WILL GET SAME GREAT
PLEASURE OUT OF SEEING THIS PICTURE AS I DID IN PLAY-
ING IN IT-

CLARK GABLE.

STARTING AT GILLIOZ THEATRE SUNDAY MARCH 11th.

Gable Telegram.

but receives a second chance from his uncle, who leaves him a department store—provided that the store show a profit within three months. Persevering with the help of a pretty store secretary, Denny's character succeeds in outwitting the store manager, who plots against him.

Had the best been saved for last? As if making an on-stage introduction, the *Souvenir Book* reads, "Carl Laemmle Presents Reginald Denny...." In the 1920s a cult of personality surrounded the corporate executives, managers, producers, and booking agents as well as the actors on stage and in film. (For a notable instance, the most famous person associated with Florence Ziegfeld's Follies was Ziegfeld himself.) The Gillioz was thus anxious to tout its connections with Universal's famous owner.

ℵ ℵ

The Gillioz Theatre's courtship of the Ozarks' Queen City had thus officially, auspiciously, begun. Even its theatrical rivals wished it well. The Electric (a block away on the northeast corner of the Square) ran an ad in the October 10 *Leader:* "The Gillioz Theatre," the Electric management writes, "Is a Credit to Our City. We Welcome You and Wish You Success." The "New Landers" (so-called for its remodeling in 1922) offered its own "Howdy Neigh-

bor," extending "the glad-hand to the Management of the new Gillioz." On November 8 the Kiwanis Club presented its annual musical revue and minstrel show at the theater. Featuring a local cast of two hundred, the show was directed by Chris Ming of the Ming Producing Company, Houston, Texas. Much like Denny's *Take it From Me,* the Gillioz Theatre Beautiful looked forward to its own happy ending, winning the girl (let's call her, allegorically, the lovely Miss Springfield Audience) and turning a quick profit. Should this dream come true, the theater would owe its success to the man who built it— M. E. Gillioz—and to where and how it was built. These form the subjects of our next chapter.

M. E. Gillioz.

2. Gillioz: The Man and His "Theatre Beautiful"

"Local Company Plans Theater on St. Louis Street," ran a front-page headline in the March 31, 1924 *Springfield Leader:*

A new motion picture and vaudeville theater, to cost approximately $150,000, will be erected on St. Louis Street near the Woodruff building by a corporation which is being organized by Frank E. Headley and a group of other prominent local business men, Mr. Headley announced yesterday.... it is expected that definite building plans will be announced within a short time....

According to preliminary plans, which have been drafted by Earl Hawkins and Company, local architects, the new play house will front on St. Louis street at the present location of the Famous Cleaning Company, just two doors west of the Woodruff Building, and will extend back to Olive street. The theater will seat 2,000 persons.

The new play house will be known as the "Gayety," and will have two entrances, Mr. Headley stated. The main lobby, which will be handsomely furnished, will face St. Louis street, and will occupy the entire present building. In this section of the building will be located the main box office, drawing room and rest rooms.

The secondary entrance will be located on Olive street, which is being widened to a 60-foot paved thoroughfare, affording large parking space for patrons of the new theater.

The men interested in the project will open offices downtown this week ... and building plans will be rushed, Mr. Headley stated.... It is known that representatives of several large motion picture corporations have been in Springfield recently in the interest of building a large theater in the downtown business district. It is understood that the desired location could not be secured.

Some of Frank Headley's announced plans panned out. Some did not. "A new motion picture and vaudeville theater" fronting St. Louis was indeed built, though it

"Local Company Plans Theater."

wasn't named the "Gayety," and it would seat 1,120 persons, not 2,000. It bore little resemblance to the artist's original sketch. (See figure: "Local Company Plans Theater.") Instead of a local firm, United Studios of Chicago (assisted by Chicago interior designer, M. R. DeHart) designed it. And it cost twice the anticipated sum. Not mentioned in the *Leader* article was its general contractor, M. E. Gillioz, for whom the theater would be named, as he had built it "with his own men and paid for it with his own money" (Rainey 25).

"Supremely aggressive, determined, original, self-reliant, generous, loyal to his friends and eternally youthful" (2): thus Albert Waters described his long-time friend, M. E. Gillioz. (See figure: M. E. Gillioz.) Gillioz had won similar friends across Missouri. Winning, after all, was his specialty, whether the prize be an influen-

Gillioz Theatre in Monett.

tial friend, a construction bid, or a political appointment. He was a self-made man, living confirmation of the reality of the American Dream. "He like[d] to make money," Waters added, "and he [didn't] mind putting it into circulation" (2). It seemed he could buy whatever he wanted: half a town even, as some in Monett (where his construction company eventually settled) would occasionally grouch while glancing over their shoulders.

As a young man, Maurice Ernest Gillioz (1877-1962) left his Swiss father's farm in Dillon (near Rolla, Missouri) for St. Louis, to work for the Frisco Railroad. Rising quickly through the ranks to construction foreman and superintendent, M. E. was transferred to Pierce City, a small railroad town six miles west of Monett, where he started his own construction business on the side. Eventually leaving the Frisco, he built miles of road with the aid of horses and mules. A stoutly built man, M. E. had no fear of hard labor, priding himself on outworking his employees. By 1914 he had moved his construction company to Pierce City's larger neighbor, Monett. Turning from roads to dam- and bridge-building, Gillioz traded his mules for heavy equipment. Scattered across Arkansas and Missouri, his sturdy, well-built bridges featured either all-concrete or steel truss construction.

Shrewdly, Gillioz applied his steel and concrete bridge-building techniques to the construction of large public buildings, including the Laclede County Courthouse, the Monett City Hall, Springfield's Lincoln and Pipkin schools, and Springfield's Medical Arts Building. He would build Joplin's Fox Theatre and (financed with his own money) the Gillioz Theatre in Monett. (See figure: Gillioz Theatre in Monett). He would build and own numerous other of Monett's prominent businesses, including the Gillioz Bank, the Gillioz Clothing Store, the Gillioz Motor Company, the Gillioz Implement Company, the Gillioz Paint and Body Shop, and the Gillioz Office Building. More than the largest contractor in Southwest Missouri, he had become a prominent banker, auto dealer, theater owner.... At the time of his passing, M. E. towered over the town's economics and politics.

M. E. was a tireless worker, a hard drinker, and a shrewd dealer who often conducted business near the open "boot" or trunk of his Duesenberg, in which he kept a bar stocked with his own private-label whiskey, "Old M. E." When bidding on a construction job he would talk shop for a while and then invite everyone outside to his car for a "break," where he would ply a different mode of persuasion. "Generous" and "loyal to his friends," as Waters declared, M. E. regaled Monett with lavish parties thrown annually on his birthday. An entertainer at heart, he was an accomplished amateur accordionist. During and after the Great Depression he would open Monett's Gillioz Theatre on Christmas Day, giving each child free admission, candy, and a shiny new quarter. Many in Monett still remember his munificence. Indeed the image of M. E. chauffeured through town in the back of his sleek, powerful twelve-cylinder Duesenberg has yet to fade from the town's collective memory. (See insert: Monett Remembers M. E.)

The stories that still circulate of his drinking, his womanizing, his bending if not breaking of rules were typical of the times: men of such power and wealth *were supposed* to use the same for their pleasure. Of course he made enemies. Yet the applause given him on opening night was both loud and largely genuine, as M. E. had achieved more than even the brashest, most optimistic in his audience could imagine for themselves: having built his own grand palace, M. E. had gained membership into the great, glamorous American entertainment industry. And the American entertainment industry of the 1920s—like American society in general—worshiped success: "the star system, the lavish architecture of its theaters ... the pride with which it disclosed the financial manipulations of its circuits and syndicates, all pointed to a set of common assumptions about the desirability of making money, amassing it, and living richly off the proceeds" (M7). On that evening, Gillioz was himself the star. He had reached his dream and, by means of his theater, offered fantasy-images of the American Dream to audiences.

The whisper of scandal surrounding the death of his secretary (his chauffeur crashed the Duesenberg with her and M. E. in the back seat) did little harm to his

Monett Remembers M. E. *John Derouche, who grew up in Monett, heard the following twice-told tale from old-timers. Of course M. E. was a football fan, and he often drove—well, sped—through neighboring towns on his way to Monett High football games. (His construction company hired workers from across the state, and having a big, strong, high-school aged son never hurt a person's chances for employment. How such practices may have cost Monett a state championship is another tale too long for telling here.) Pulled over, M. E. found himself before a judge who didn't take kindly to this rich man in his big car speeding through town. Fined a whopping $500, M.E. tugged a wad of bills from his pocket and tossed $1,000 on the table, saying, "And I'll be coming back through in three hours. Don't bother stopping me." While sounding like the punch line of an old joke, the story shows how Monett remembers its most famous, most affluent citizen.*

business and political career. A prominent figure in the Grand Old Party, he was a Missouri delegate to the 1932 Republican Convention. "Supremely aggressive, determined, original, self-reliant," M. E. was exactly the right man in the right place at the right time to build the Gillioz Theatre in Springfield.

ⵣ ⵣ ⵣ ⵣ ⵣ ⵣ ⵣ ⵣ ⵣ ⵣ ⵣ ⵣ ⵣ ⵣ

As the March 31, 1924 *Leader* article remarked, "several large motion picture corporations" had tried to build such a theater themselves. "The desired location," however, "could not be secured." (Just as vaudeville booking agencies had their own "circuits," so each motion picture corporation distributed to its own "chain" of leased theaters. The presence of rival theaters in downtown Springfield represented the competition among distributors.) Evidently the Gillioz partnership succeeded where these larger outside corporations had failed. Yet the manner of their success created a legacy of future legal problems. For the Gillioz Theatre consisted of two properties: the house proper, which occupied an entire block on Olive Street, and the theater entrance, which occupied a narrow storefront on St. Louis Street. The Gillioz partnership purchased the Olive Street property. Unable to purchase the St. Louis Street storefront, they were forced to lease it. (This arrangement—in effect, a dual ownership of the theater properties—hindered the building's later restoration until 1989 when Jim D. Morris, local businessman and philanthropist, managed to purchase the storefront property, ultimately deeding the theater to the Springfield Landmarks Preservation Trust.) Though signing a hundred-year lease would have proved distasteful to a man used to having his way, it was the only means by which Gillioz and his partnership could reach its prize: a theater entrance on Route 66. It didn't hurt that the Woodruff (Springfield's largest office building) stood just two doors to the east and the Netter's just next door to the west. They completed the financial formula for a successful urban theater: one drove into town for business, shopping, and an evening's entertainment. (See insert: The Springfield Hospitality Club.) The Netter's Department Store and other fashionable shops nearby attracted a well-heeled clientele. The Gillioz wasn't isolated economically from its neighbors, but drew on their prosperity. And they drew, in turn, on the Gillioz. (This same economic interdependence would later doom the Gillioz when the downtown fell on hard times.)

The Springfield Hospitality Club. *Occasionally throughout the late 1920s the Hospitality Club (precursor to the Springfield Convention and Visitors Bureau) ran newspaper ads aimed at increasing downtown business. These targeted the outlying towns and countryside. As the* Daily News *ad for February 1, 1929 reads, "To Springfield Folks: Mail this page to an out-of-town friend." (See figure: "All Around the Town.") This particular ad sends a mixed message, in that it touts the city's down-home hospitality—"that undefinable spirit that makes visitors feel at home in Springfield"—while presenting an exaggerated image of a metropolis city-scape, as if Springfield were more Chicago than Chicago. Yet the real come-on of this ad (like others run by the Hospitality Club) is a listing of entertainments at the downtown theaters: the Electric, Jefferson, and Landers were featuring movies and live-variety vaudeville, while the Gillioz showed a feature movie and Vitaphone-film vaudeville.*

The Leader *ad for August 2, 1928 makes explicit the formula for economic success: encouraging day-trips to Springfield for shopping and a movie. Along with a listing of five theaters (the Electric, Jefferson, Gillioz, and Landers, plus the Mullikin), the ad makes the following pitch to parents of school-aged children:*

Do This For Them
BEFORE SCHOOL STARTS

Vacation ends next week for thousands of young Southwest Missourians.... The opportunity of enjoying themselves in Springfield this summer is fast ebbing. Just one more week available for their entertainment.

Plan to bring them to the pleasure center of Southwest Missouri on one or more of these days to see Springfield at its best.... You, too, will be glad to spend the day or weekend in Springfield. Put aside all else and come!

Combine business with pleasure.

A survey of the stores reveals that they are filled with things the youngsters still want for school wear. You will enjoy shopping in the Springfield stores. The styles and variety are satisfactory—and the prices are exceedingly low.

The building would thus be an "L" in shape, fat along one end, thin down the other, the biggest part owned, the most important part leased. Yet the architectural compromise of a long, narrow lobby entrance leading to a larger, wider house wasn't unique to the Gillioz; it was a common arrangement for America's urban theaters. As theater historian Albert F. McLean writes, "whereas the European playhouses generally stood isolated on sizable plots of ground, the vaudeville palaces had to be squeezed into the valuable real estate left between large department stores and commercial offices in downtown areas" (M196). In this respect the Gillioz compares to Boston's New Theatre:

> Built in 1894, Keith's celebrated New Theatre in Boston met the problem of crowding a theater onto a narrow lot by a concentrated variety of ornamental detail on the front of the theater and by a system of foyers and lobbies which whetted the expectations of the audience as it approached the house proper. The narrow frontage ... was covered with a plentitude of decorative detail— ornamental iron work, stained glass, pediments, cornices, and incandescent lighting—proclaim-

"All Around the Town."

22

ing loudly the presence of Amusement among the stolid, work-weary faces of hotels, department stores, and office buildings. (M196)

The Gillioz, too, squeezed itself into the "valuable real estate left between large department stores and commercial offices" (here, between the Netter's and the Woodruff), piled as much "ornamental detail" as it could upon its narrow frontage, and built a "system of foyers and lobbies" extending a whopping 120 feet in total, aimed at whetting "the expectations of the audience as it approached the house proper." All worked according to formula.

The Gillioz cost $300,000, of which $75,000 was spent on furnishing the interior. In today's real dollars, the building would have cost $3.5 million. Yet dollar equivalents between 1926 and 2006 never seem to balance. If built today, the Gillioz could *never* be completed for a mere $3.5 million. At the time of writing, the theater's restoration had already cost $5.5 million. Indeed, architects working on the renovation have suggested (perhaps without exaggerating) that it would cost about as much to restore as it would to demolish and haul away the thousands of tons of steel, brick, and concrete. Like the man's trademark bridges, his theater would have had to be blown up; it couldn't be simply, easily knocked down. As one might expect, much is hidden underneath the terra-cotta façade and plaster interior. The build-

ing's inner construction is as interesting as its decorated surface, though for opposite reasons. Being a bridge-builder, Gillioz applied all that he had learned about heavy construction. In a sense, he "over-built" his theater, using twelve-inch steel I-beams and load-bearing masonry everywhere in the upper flooring. Such steel-and-concrete construction undergirds both the massive balcony and delicate-seeming mezzanine, creating a sense of openness and airiness throughout. Excepting the doors, hand railings, seating, and lobby furniture, there is no wood in his Theatre Beautiful. Of course it had a fire curtain, emblazoned with Gillioz's signature "G." His theater might catch fire but, unlike the stately Baldwin, it could never burn down.

In an average Midwest town of 1923, "about two and three-fourths times the city's entire population attended the motion picture theaters during the month of July, ... the 'valley' month of the year, and four and one-half times the total population in the 'peak' month of December" (LL263). The cause of this summer "valley" or drop in attendance (thus, in profit) was room temperature. Prior to air conditioning, a crowded summer theater would have been sweltering. (For this reason, the traditional "legitimate" theater season ran from autumn to spring.) The Gillioz Theatre's décor acknowledged the changing seasons in subtle ways. For example, lining the outer lobby's walls were large, four-foot by one-foot art-deco light fixtures, each containing four colors of bulbs. In fall and winter, the fixtures' red and yellow bulbs were lit, giving an air of warmth; in spring and summer, the blue and green bulbs were lit, giving an air of coolness. Yet lighting did little to keep the sweat off patrons' brows.

While the Gillioz advertised itself as being "Cool as a Cave" in the summer of 1927, an innovative cooling system was installed in 1928, "the first such system for Southwest Missouri, and one said to rival anything in New York, Chicago, St. Louis, or Kansas City" (Rainey 35). Costing $35,000, it was in fact a "swamp" or evaporative cooling system. Springfieldian Charley Talley remembers "working for J. B. McCarthy Plumbing and Heating in 1949," when they "put in a 5-by-8-foot coil" in the Gillioz, "the biggest," Talley notes, "that I'd ever seen. We hooked it up to the theater's cold well water. Then we directed a big fan at the coil to cool the theater" (Billings 4B). The new coil must have improved an already efficient system: by its July 4, 1941 showing of *The Shepherd of the Hills*, the theater was advertising itself as the "Air Conditioned Gillioz." Of course, from the 1920s through to the 1960s (when many homes afforded their own) a theater's air conditioning was itself a draw, luring people out of the summer heat.

Talley's reference to "the theater's cold well water"

also connects the Gillioz to a hidden natural resource of significance to the city's very founding. Just north of the theater, across the street from Founder's Park, a public marker commemorates the 1829 founding of Springfield. As Harris Dark and Phyllis Dark describe it,

> After some time in the area, hunting and inspecting the countryside, the Campbells traveled up the James [River] a few miles, and went overland a few more miles. They found four springs that united to form Wilson's Creek, and in the center of the area of springs they discovered what later was called a "bottomless spring" or a "natural well of wonderful depth," and here they made their claim in the custom of the frontier—they carved their initials on a large ash tree. That act came to be accepted as the founding of Springfield. (DD25)

In the cellar beneath the Gillioz stage, workers had drilled a well down into the Springfield aquifer, as this "bottomless spring" came to be called. Hidden beneath the house seats were a series of small grates and shallow ventilation caps; these opened to air ducts underneath the concrete flooring, which led back to the cellar fan. Quietly, then, and largely undetected by audiences, the Gillioz Theatre's "swamp cooler" offered respite from the Ozarks' summer swelter.

Moving from the cellar to the projection room (from the theater's belly, as it were, to its brain and nerve center) we find further technology that the October 10, 1926 *Springfield Republican* described as state-of-the-art: "unusually large," the projection room was "excellently equipped with two [projection] machines, a slide projector, automatic rewind equipment and a fire-proof container for film." The machines "have been adjusted with all possible care so that the best possible projection may be obtained. In order to further this end, a silver leaf screen has been secured, which assures a strong and steady picture." Though the *Leader* termed it "unusually large," people laboring in the room would have found it anything but cozy.

"It must have been hotter than hell in here, and not just in August," remarked a board member of the Springfield Landmarks Preservation Trust. It was 1990, and the Trust's founding members were completing a tour of the building they had just acquired. Standing at the top of the dusty balcony, they peered past a solid, galvanized-steel door into the dark, cramped projection room. Usually locked from the inside, the door not only kept sounds inside from reaching the audience; it also kept fires from spreading, and fires were a theater's worst enemy. (The early nitrate-based film was liable to catch fire if the projector ran too slowly or stopped: in 1932 the Elite Theater in Nixa burned to the ground after the film jammed, caught fire, and the flames spread through the house.) The October 10, 1926

Republican declared the Gillioz projection room "exceptionally well-ventilated, air being exchanged every three minutes, thus providing for escape of any poisonous gas which may arise from the film." Ventilated perhaps, but hardly air-conditioned; perhaps the two small windows on the south wall allowed an occasional breeze.

Under the windows was a narrow shelf, where the two film winders and a splicing block sat. Here the projectionist would rewind the film reels to get ready for the next show. He could also repair breaks in the film, as well as insert newsreels and other, shorter footage within larger reels. All of the usable equipment had been removed by 1980, but there was still a lot of stuff: an RCA Stereo sound amplifier, the switch to open and close the stage curtain, a phone to the manager's office, parts of an old projector (vintage 1940s), some empty reel canisters, and two massive metal 35mm projector housings that had been bolted to the floor. Though vented through ports in the ceiling, the projectors would have thrown off heavy heat. And among the carcasses of pigeons littering the floor were the burnt ends of spent welding rods.

Until the 1950s, when a safer xenon arc light was developed, there were no incandescent lamps powerful enough to throw an image across the cavernous auditorium. So, films were illuminated by white-hot arc rods (similar to welders' rods), which the projectionist had continually to trim as they burned, in order to keep the light source constant. In addition to the brilliant light, the arc rods put out a tremendous heat and an acrid air. When a rod was used up the projectionist removed the end from the projector with metal pliers, dropped the hot piece on the concrete floor, and got a fresh one from a metal container on the back of the projector base. He put it in the projector, trimmed it to the proper length, and fired it up. He did all this while the second projector continued showing film. He then threaded the next reel into the idle projector and waited for a signal in one of the movie's frames to give the exact second when to switch projectors and continue the film. If the projectionist did his job well (and most in the Gillioz did), the audience never knew when the switch was made. No wonder that the theater's 1926 *Souvenir Book* touted the projectionist, Jess Tuckness, among its vital "House Personnel."

It goes without saying that a building's architecture reflects its intended use, which in the case of the Gillioz is obviously a theater. But what sort? (See insert: Springfield's Downtown Theaters.) Returning to the 1924 *Leader* article, we read of plans for "a new motion picture and vaudeville theater." It is this combination (that is, of "motion picture and vaudeville") in this order (the motion picture first, vaudeville second) that marks the Gillioz as a "combination" or "transition" theater, one built during the ascendence of film and the twilight of vaudeville.

Though marking its "centennial celebration in 1926"

(S232), vaudeville's days were numbered. Writing in *The Nation* in July 1929, theater critic Alexander Bakshy weighed vaudeville's "prosperity in the provincial and often very backward localities" against its collapse in New York and other major cities. He writes, "The decline of vaudeville in New York revealed itself earlier in the closing down of such Broadway houses as Tony Pastor's, Hammerstein's, and the Colonial. Now comes the downfall of that greatest house of spectacle—the Hippodrome" (S232-33). As Bakshy notes, "the largest nation-wide vaudeville enterprise—the Radio-Keith-Orpheum circuit—operates about 700 theaters served by 25,000 artists and having an average weekly attendance of some 12,000,000 people" (S233). Yet "it must be admitted," Bakshy continues, "that only five out of the 700 theaters, namely one each in New York, Pittsburgh, Chicago, Los Angeles, and San Francisco, serve their public with 'straight' vaudeville":

> All the others divide their program between vaudeville and movies. But though the concession of half the program to the movies was undoubtedly a tribute to a rival power which was rapidly becoming more formidable, today it signifies no more than the desire to provide an entertainment of real variety. In fact until the appearance of the talking pictures the gains were entirely on the side of vaudeville, which even invaded the movie houses and drove the pictures to a position of acknowledged inferiority. (S233)

We doubt that 1920s Springfield would have included itself among those "provincial ... localities." As Bakshy notes, all but five of the 700 RKO theaters "divide[d] their program between vaudeville and movies." Bakshy tries to put a game face on for vaudeville, explaining this division as "no more than the desire to provide an entertainment of real variety." But the Gillioz partnership had read the writing on the wall. (See insert: Springfield's Downtown Theaters.)

In 1926, the Gillioz Theatre's three major downtown rivals were the Landers, the Jefferson, and the Electric. (For newspaper accounts of their respective openings, see Appendices.) Opened in 1909, the Landers was built for "legitimate" theater, as evidenced by the depth of its stage. Including a 6-foot apron extending in front of the proscenium curtain, the stage offered a thirty-six foot deep, thirty-two foot wide acting space, with an additional six-foot depth behind the back curtain: some forty-two feet total. With twelve-foot wings on either

Springfield's Downtown Theaters. *Some thirty theaters operated in Springfield from 1900 through the 1930s, most concentrated on or near the Public Square or north on Commercial Street and Boonville Avenue. Many were small and jury-rigged, converted from storefronts or warehouses. Given the intense competition (each new opening cut into the others' business), some were short-lived, closing after a few marginally profitable years. Most showed films; some showed vaudeville; many showed a combination of both.*

Considering just theaters on or near the Public Square, the Star (opened 1905) on Boonville showed primarily vaudeville, though it was the city's first to show "kinodrome" pictures. The Lyric (opened 1907, renamed the Peoples Theatre in 1912) on College Street and the Majestic (opened 1909, renamed the Aladdin in 1910) on South Avenue were nickelodeons. Built for "legitimate" theater, the Landers-Orpheum (opened 1909, seating 900) on Walnut Street showed both vaudeville and movies. A converted skating rink, the Jefferson (opened 1911, seating 1,400) on South Jefferson Avenue and McDaniel Street showed vaudeville and some movies; so did the Electric (opened 1916, seating 1,100) on the northeast corner of the Public Square. A resplendent vaudeville palace, the Baldwin (opened 1891, seating 1,500) on Saint Louis Street would have topped them all in luxury—the Gillioz included—had it not burned in 1909. (See figures: The Landers Theatre, Jefferson Theatre, Electric Theatre, and Baldwin Theatre.)

Among downtown theaters, the Gillioz was thus Springfield's newest and grandest—at least until 1948, when the Jewell (that is, the old Jefferson Theatre, refurbished and renamed) opened as a movie house, becoming home in 1955 to the nationally-telecast Ozark Jubilee. We have yet to mention the Springfield Convention Hall (opened 1913) on McDaniel Street and Campbell Avenue, which "was the major site of big musical events" through the 1920s (G108), and the Shrine Mosque (opened 1923, seating 2,300 with additional fold-up seating totalling 4,500) on the corner of Saint Louis Street and Kimbrough Avenue. (See figure: Shrine Mosque.)

It's hard to imagine the sheer capacity of these combined theaters. In total, the four major houses—the Landers, the Jefferson, the Electric, and the Gillioz—could seat 4,520. Throw in the Shrine Mosque seating and, assuming a population of 50,000, some twenty percent of Springfield's residents could have attended a downtown performance on any given evening.

side, the Landers stage was capable of serious dramatic and operatic performances. Hence, Bakshy's point holds true for the Landers: "until the appearance of the talking

Landers Theatre.

pictures," this Walnut Street theater disdained the poor-quality "photoplays" showing in smaller nickelodeons. Yet a fire in 1919 ruined the entire backstage (the auditorium was spared through the asbestos fire curtain), leading to the Landers' modernization. When the theater reopened in 1922 it sported a new, fully equipped projection room, and movies would be its major fare through the coming decades.

In fact the Landers was the first of Springfield's theaters to wire itself for sound. In 1928, when Al Jolson's *Jazz Singer* played, the Landers became the first house in the city and the thirty-fifth in the nation (Langely 8B) to show this partially-talking Vitaphone film. When the movie breaks from silent film to "talkie," Jolson's character says the following famous words—the first that Springfield's theatergoers would hear on screen:

Wait a minute, wait a minute, you ain't heard nothin' yet! Wait a minute, I tell ya! You ain't heard nothin'! You wanna hear "Toot, Toot, Tootsie"? All right, hold on, hold on. (Walks back to one of the band members) Lou, listen. Play "Toot, Toot, Tootsie," Three chorus, you understand. In the third chorus, I whistle. Now give it to 'em hard and heavy, go right ahead. (Band starts playing. Sings)

Toot, Toot, Tootsie goo'bye,
Toot, Toot, Tootsie don't cry!
The choo-choo train that takes me away from
          you,
No words can tell how sad it makes me!
Kiss me, Tootsie, and then
Do it over again.
Watch for the mail,
I'll never fail,
If you don't get a letter then you'll know I'm in
          jail.
Toot, Toot, Tootsie don't cry,
Toot, Toot, Tootsie goo'bye!

The Landers would follow with *The Hometowners* (music by George M. Cohan), the city's first all-talking movie (DD99-100). Ironically, the 1919 fire proved an economic blessing in disguise, allowing the Landers to compete for audiences by means of the latest film technology.

Like the Gillioz, the Jefferson and the Electric were both "combination" theaters, showing film and vaudeville together (though, through the 1920s, vaudeville predominated on their stages). Originally a skating rink, the Jefferson was spacious and handsomely appointed; though the building was razed in 1961, contemporary photographs show a fairly deep stage whose acting space was sufficient for live performance. The Electric's stage was forty feet wide and a somewhat shallow twenty-eight feet deep. It had no pit, so the eight-piece "Electric Orchestra" played on the auditorium floor in front of the stage apron. Like the Gillioz, it owned a "Mighty Wurlitzer."

☙ ☙

The Gillioz was thus a relative latecomer to Springfield's theater scene. It boasted the latest technology, though management had to scramble in 1928 to match the Landers' wiring for sound. (Until its 1980 closing, this was perhaps the last time that another city theater would beat the Gillioz to a new film technology.) Of the four downtown theaters, its stage was the least suited to live performance, being thirty-eight feet wide and a mere twenty feet in depth. This shallowness brought the movie screen closer to the audience; it also made for a cramped upstage and little room for dramatic scenery. The wings (twenty feet stage right, eighteen feet stage left) were large enough, though the orchestra pit—with the organ console squeezed into the right hand corner, the piano into the left—was not. Nine feet deep at its center, the pit narrowed sharply toward either wing, making it too cramped for more than a seven- or eight-piece orchestra. Then again, the house Wurlitzer made enough sound for silent film. In the basement, the Gillioz had several dressing rooms, each just large enough for a makeup table and chair.

Within a year of its opening the theater would drop all

Jefferson Theatre.

Electric Theatre.

Baldwin Theatre.

Shrine Mosque.

pretenses to vaudeville, leaving live-variety to its rivals. Declaring November 1927 "'Better Pictures' Month," the Gillioz management presented its business decision in the guise of an advertising campaign. Interviewed in the October 9, 1927 *Leader*, the manager explains: "Instead of mixing pictures with vaudeville orchestra numbers and other features we intend hereafter to use the money these features would cost in buying feature pictures. We are convinced pictures are wanted above everything else and that being the case, we intend to give Springfield the best we can get." We needn't doubt that "pictures" were "wanted above everything else," though we might glimpse a larger economic picture beyond the price of films. On a daily basis one "feature" picture, one projectionist, and one organist cost less—probably significantly less over an entire season—than live acts and a seven- or eight-piece orchestra paid union-scale wages. By January 1928 the theater had switched from Universal to the Midland Circuit; A. H. Bachman was out as manager, replaced by Vogel Gettier. The changes suggest

some struggle to make ends meet. (As the Gillioz *Souvenir Book* declared, "The mission of a theater is to entertain." Put another way, its mission is to make money.)

"'Better Pictures' Month" notwithstanding, the Gillioz remained very much a live theater, its most historic, public moments occurring on stage. (Of course, equally memorable private moments occurred offstage in the darkened auditorium, outside in the lobbies' brightness, and upstairs in the cramped, hot projection room.) Thus our history divides, like the "combination" theater that the Gillioz was, into two strains, the live acts that opened the theater and continued intermittently through to the 1950s, and the films that came increasingly to dominate, turning toward the end into the theater's exclusive fare.

Before turning to these we might detour briefly through the tumultuous decade that gave birth to the Gillioz, the Roaring Twenties. Admittedly, what follows reads like a history lesson. If you don't want to go to school, feel free to play hooky from this next chapter.

3. Springfield, the Roaring Twenties, and the Technologies of Leisure

The young seem to be obsessed by jazz and a merry round of dance and by movies and autos—a flapper, a flask, and a flivver.... Modern youth has outdistanced every former generation.... They do not hesitate to break with tradition....

They have so many more opportunities than the old folks had. The universe is changed, the discoveries and inventions of science have released forces which are at their disposal and through which they can either make or mar civilization....
—Dr. Charles E. Schaffer, July 17, 1920 *Frederick (MD) Post*

If you would avoid temptation to attend the movies, don't read their advertisements, don't gaze at the gaudy outside display, don't loiter near the theater doors. Would you lose the desire for worldly dance? Then stop listening to radio jazz, burn your dance records, and stay away from the alluring ballroom....
—M. J. McClellan, May 30, 1926 *Christ's Ambassadors: A Paper for the Young People* (Springfield, Missouri)

In recent years it has been the fashion to deplore the loose conduct of the younger generation.... You cannot compare youth of today with the youth of yesterday in this respect, for young people in your time ... were not beset by such liberty and licence as we now give the movies....
—Dr. William Brady, July 9, 1928 *Lima (OH) News*

Less than a month before the Gillioz Theatre's October 1926 opening, the city of Springfield was caught up in a debate over theater and morality—specifically, over movie showings on Sunday, which had been prohibited by city ordinance since December 1921. The December 16, 1926 *Springfield Leader* summarized the debate:

The move to close theaters on Sunday in Spring-

field was launched in the fall of 1921 following a series of revival meetings conducted by Bob Jones, Alabama evangelist. The Ministerial Alliance and Protestant Christian Council, both of this city, later sponsored the campaign for [the ban. A motion] requesting the city council to pass an ordinance prohibiting Sunday shows was presented to the city commissioners.

Founder of Bob Jones University, the "Alabama evangelist" had evidently struck a nerve. Though the city council "refused to pass such an ordinance by a vote of three to two," the Ministerial Alliance pressed its case, presenting a petition for a city-wide referendum. On December 27, 1921, a large majority voted to adopt the ordinance banning Sunday shows. Over the next five years Springfieldians would vote twice more to uphold the ban.

Yet on Sunday, September 19, 1926, W. W. Smith publicly challenged the ordinance. A colorful soul, Smith owned the Grand, a nickelodeon tucked into the southwest corner of the Public Square. The December 16 *Leader* article recounted his arrest:

The preceding day Smith had announced that he would attempt to open on Sunday, so Chief of Police A. C. Boehm and several of his officers were on hand Sunday afternoon when the show opened. They allowed Smith to make a fifteen minute address to the crowd and run the picture for seven minutes before they closed the theater and arrested the owner and two of his employees.

Convicted in municipal court, Smith appealed his case. On December 15, 1926, Criminal Court Judge Warren L. White ruled in Smith's favor, citing ways that the ordinance discriminated "against the theater and in favor of the same class of entertainment if conducted apart from the theater." Though City Attorney Dan Nee vowed to fight on, Springfield's theaters stayed open.

Should the Ministerial Alliance have worried so over

the influence of Sunday theater? And not just of movies but of Sunday vaudeville, Sunday radio, Sunday car rides, and the new styles of Sunday music, "ragtime" and jazz? The fact is, theaters did more than compete with churches for attendance on Sunday: the new, increasingly wealthy and influential "entertainment industry" was subtly, pervasively reshaping American urban culture, centering its citizens' lives around leisure and, thus, around the technologies of leisure—in particular, the automobile, the moving picture, and the radio. How a city, how a nation spends its leisure time (and its leisure dollars) tells us much about its culture and character.

Let's begin by noting that "leisure time" and "vacation time" remain inventions of the 1920s. "'Vacations in 1890?' echoed one substantial citizen. 'Why, the word wasn't in the dictionary!'" (LL261). As Robert S. Lynd and Helen Merrell Lynd suggest,

> Middletown people today enjoy a greater variety of these alternate other things than their parents knew a generation ago.... [Leisure time's] more striking aspects relate to the coming of inventions, the automobile, the movies, radio, that have swept through the community since 1890, dragging the life of the city in their wake. (LL225-26)

To the previous generation, such "alternate other things" as vacations were unheard of: unless ill or disabled, one worked six days a week and the seventh belonged to the Lord. But no longer were Americans compelled to scratch out a living from dawn to dusk. Increased affluence, urbanization, and the accessibility of modern technologies allowed people of all classes the precious "free" time that they could "spend" at their leisure, for their own entertainment. The dominant metaphor here—that of "spending" time, as if days were dimes, weeks dollars—attests to life's economic basis. Only with sufficient wealth does one have time to "spend" on entertainment; the flip side of this same coin is, of course, the developing technologies and "business" of entertainment. (See insert: Springfield and Middletown.)

The Gillioz and other urban theaters opened to entertain. They opened to make money, too. The nature of theater entertainment and its impact—moral as well as economic—on 1920s Springfield, our own Middletown, thus forms the subject of this chapter.

ᴧᴧ ᴧᴧ ᴧᴧ ᴧᴧ ᴧᴧ ᴧᴧ ᴧᴧ ᴧᴧ ᴧᴧ ᴧᴧ

The Roaring Twenties was an exhilarating, nervous decade for Springfield as it was for Middletown and most other towns of the American Midwest, a decade of unprecedented growth in population,

in affluence, in aspirations, in urban-social problems. By 1926, Springfield had finally surpassed its commercial rival, Joplin, in size and economic clout. The city's population was nearing 50,000. Like so many other Midwestern cities, Springfield owed much of its prosperity to the train and to transportation generally. Four railroads served the city: the Kansas City-Memphis, the Missouri Pacific, the Kansas City, Clinton, and Springfield, and the St. Louis and San Francisco—that is, the mighty Frisco, whose 2,800 employees made it the city's biggest employer (Holsen 230). In 1926 the Frisco Line touted its big, brand new passenger station. Thirty-two passenger trains passed through daily and trolley tracks crisscrossed the town. Though air flight remained a novelty in 1926, work on the fifty-acre McCluer Flying Field had begun the previous summer; built on the J. W. McCluer farm east of Glenstone Avenue, the facility would offer commercial passenger service by 1929, growing into Springfield's Municipal Airport (DD92, 98).

While the city's commerce ran on rail, its leisure industry rode on the newfangled asphalt-macadam. As Lynd and Lynd write, "at the close of 1923 there were 6,221 passenger cars" in Middletown, that is, "roughly two for every three families" (LL253). As a status symbol, the automobile's lure was irresistible. "At the turn of the century, business-class people began to feel apologetic if they did not have a telephone" (LL253); by the mid-1920s the automobile, too, had "reached the point of being an accepted essential of normal living" (LL253). It had certainly become an "essential" for Springfieldians: in his *Economic Survey of Missouri* (1927), James N. Holsen estimates that forty-eight percent of the city's 14,000 families owned telephones while seventy-three percent owned automobiles (88). (See figure: Cars on the Public Square, 1927.) Quite likely, the city's cars outnumbered its household bathtubs.

Car ownership placed tremendous strain on family budgets, driving many to mortgage their homes for their auto. "I'll go without food before I'll see us give up

---

Springfield and Middletown. In *Middletown: A Study of American Culture*, social-anthropologists Robert S. Lynd and Helen Merrell Lynd examined urban life in the mid-1920s, describing a typical mid-sized town of 38,000 and the economic, domestic, social, political, religious, and—most important for our purposes—leisure-time practices of its citizens. In searching for "Middletown," as they named their sample community, Lynd and Lynd looked for such features as a "temperate climate," an "industrial culture with modern high-speed machine production," a "substantial local artistic life," and a "rapid rate of growth" leading to an "assortment of the growing pains accompanying contemporary social change" (LL7). As a further criterion, their sample city "should, if possible, be in that common-denominator of America, the Middle West" (LL7-8). Their choice of town most "representative ... of contemporary American life" (7) proved to be Muncie, Indiana. Though somewhat larger than Muncie's 38,000 and nestled in the Ozarks, Springfield is much like a second Middletown. Thus, where statistics for 1920s Springfield are lacking, we have taken Lynd and Lynd's Middletown as comparable.

Cars on the Public Square, 1927.

the car" (LL256), said one Middletown woman emphatically. Still, popular advertising drove home the fantasy of leisure, pleasure, freedom, and happiness through car ownership. In summer 1924 an issue of the *Saturday Evening Post* featured "a two-page spread on the automobile, quoting a 'bank president in a Mid-Western city' as saying, '"a man who works six days a week and spends the seventh on his own doorstep certainly will not pick up the extra dimes in the great thoroughfares of life'" (LL259). "'Some sunny Sunday very soon,' said another two-page spread in the *Post*, 'just drive an Overland up to your door—tell the family to hurry the packing and get aboard—and be off with smiles down the nearest road—free, loose, and happy—bound for green wonderlands'" (LL259).

At least one Middletown preacher denounced such *"automobilitis*—the thing those people have who go off motoring on Sunday instead of going to church" (LL259). By 1923, Springfield boasted some 148 miles of street, sixty miles of it paved. But while the Ozarks saw some benefit from the Centennial Road Law of 1921—the law that "lifted Missouri out of the mud," leading to "the development of the Missouri state highway system" (DD94)—most roads leading into Springfield were still hard-riding dirt and gravel, damaging to tires and springs. There was one wonderful exception. In November 1926 America's "Main Street," soon-to-be-famous Route 66, was officially commissioned, its path cutting through Springfield's Public Square, following St. Louis Street to the east and College Street to the west. (See figure: Gillioz on Route 66.) With such a road came prospects of tourism— the ultimate leisure industry, spurring further urban growth and construction. The automobile thus played its role in developing the local leisure and tourist industry. Yet it did so, not by taking Springfieldians out to the surrounding "green wonderlands" but by bringing travelers into the city for a day's business, shopping, and an evening show. As the Chamber of Com-

The Gillioz on Route 66. It's been said that the Theatre Beautiful and our "nation's mother road" (as novelist John Steinbeck described Route 66) share the same birthday. This is almost true. The theater opened on October 11, 1926 and Route 66 was officially commissioned one month to the day later. On November 11, 1926 the U.S. Secretary of Agriculture officially approved the Federal Interstate Highway System. Reaching across 2,448 miles of America, Route 66 stretched from Chicago to Los Angeles *via* Springfield, Missouri.

When Cyrus Avery of Tulsa and John T. Woodruff of Springfield joined in promoting a designated highway route from Chicago to Los Angeles, they envisioned a road to connect towns that at the time had no interstate highway access. By September 1925 the route ran from Chicago to Bloomington and Springfield, Illinois; from Springfield to St. Louis, Rolla, Springfield, and Joplin, Missouri; from Joplin to Vinita, Tulsa, Oklahoma City, El Reno, and Sayre, Oklahoma; from Sayre to Amarillo, Texas; from Amarillo to Tucumcari, Santa Fe, Los Lunas, and Gallup, New Mexico; from Gallup to Holbrook and Flagstaff, Arizona; from Flagstaff to Barstow and, finally, Los Angeles, California. In each of these cities the road passed through the heart of the business district. In Springfield it cut straight through the Public Square, right past the Woodruff Building on St. Louis Street. John T. Woodruff knew what he was doing.

Due to Woodruff's involvement, Springfield has come to be known as the "birthplace of Route 66." That's a fair call. The seven states had to agree on a number and some wanted it named Route 60. It was Woodruff who called a meeting at his Springfield office building with Cyrus Avery and Missouri's state highway engineer, B. H. Piepmeier. At that historic meeting on April 30, 1926 the road was christened Route 66.

It wouldn't have been difficult for M. E. Gillioz to gain an insider's knowledge of the negotiations regarding the road's naming and its potential impact. After all, he was building his new theater just two doors west of Woodruff's own "skyscraper." (To modern eyes, the Woodruff Building may not seem that much; at the time, it was Springfield's largest and most modern, being the first office building nationwide to feature fluorescent lighting throughout.) For his part, Woodruff was busy building the Kentwood Arms a few blocks east, aiming to accommodate the highway's overnight travelers. It was the city's first hotel built specifically for motorists rather than rail passengers.

Woodruff continued to oversee the road's development. On February 4, 1927 he hosted a meeting of businessmen (again in his Springfield office) who formed the U.S. 66 Highway Association, aimed at promoting the new highway. After all, there was much still to do: the road itself was not entirely paved until mid-1938. At this meeting the slogan, "Main Street of America," was hit upon. Route 66 would go on to star in movies and in song, becoming the nation's most storied road.

Gillioz on Route 66.

merce touted in its promotions, "All Good Roads Lead to Springfield: The Heart of the Ozarks" (G98). (See insert: The Gillioz on Route 66.)

"Like the automobile," write Lynd and Lynd, "the motion picture is more to Middletown than simply a new way of doing an old thing; it has added new dimensions to the city's leisure" (263), particularly through its promise of escape:

> "Go to a motion picture ... and let yourself go," Middletown reads in a *Saturday Evening Post* advertisement. "Before you know it you are *living* the story—laughing, loving, hating, struggling, winning! All the adventure, all the romance, all the excitement you lack in your daily life are in— Pictures. They take you completely out of your-self into a wonderful new world.... Out of the cage of everyday existence! If only for an after-noon or an evening—escape!" (LL265)

Though the more affluent among Middletown residents went more often than its working-class families (LL264), "about ... four and one-half times the total population" of Middletown attended its "nine motion picture theaters in ... December" 1923 (LL263). While moralists worried over the numbers, equally worrisome were the movies' fantasy-themes. While western "action films" and com-edies could "draw heavy houses," it was the film "with burning 'heart interest'" that packed "Middletown's motion picture houses week after week" (LL266):

> Young Middletown enters eagerly into the vivid experience of *Flaming Youth:* "neckers, petters, white kisses, red kisses, pleasure-mad daugh-ters, sensation-craving mothers, ... the truth bold, naked, sensational"—so ran the press advertisement—under the spell of the power-

ful conditioning medium of pictures presented with music and all possible heightening of the emotional content, and the added factor of sharing this experience with a "date" in a darkened room. (LL266-67)

Such prurience in advertising would raise a blush in any self-respecting Sunday School teacher's cheek. The Gillioz featured its own sug-gestive ads (as this, from Novem-ber 11, 1928): *"See and Hear*—the underworld—night life—cabarets, Ruthless gangsters! Women, hard-boiled but beautiful! *Gang war!* ...." And yet, most worrisome was the movie house's "darkened room," where high school-aged boys and girls went on their new-fangled "dates."

Much like "vacation," the high-school "date" was pretty much an invention of the 1920s leisure and entertain-ment industry. Whereas courtship in the 1890s featured boy and girl sitting on the parlor davenport, "a 'date' at home" was now "'slow' compared with motoring, a new film, or a dance in a near-by town" (LL134). In 1890 a 'well-brought-up' boy and girl were commonly forbid-den to sit together in the dark; but motion pictures and automobiles have lifted this taboo" (LL137). (We should add that the "modern date" was made possible by the invention of the "modern woman," whose bobbed hair, flapper dress, and "scandalous" behavior expressed her new social, sexual, economic independence: an "old fashioned" girl would still have preferred the davenport to a rumble seat.) Of course the new dating-ritual cost money. "You can't have a date nowadays," wrote a Mid-dletown reporter, "without making a big hole in a five dollar bill" (LL141).

Expressing concerns that Springfield's own commu-nity leaders repeated time and again, teachers and law-makers in 1920s Middletown questioned film's pervasive influence upon the city's impressionable youth:

> Some high school teachers are convinced that the movies are a powerful factor in bringing about the "early sophistication" of the young and the relaxing of social taboos. One working class mother frankly welcomes the movies as an aid in childrearing, saying, "I send my daughter because a girl has to learn the ways of the world somehow and the movies are a good safe way." The judge of the juvenile court lists the movies as one of the "big four" causes of local juvenile delinquency.... While the community attempts to safeguard its schools from commercially intent private hands, this powerful new educational instrument,

which has taken Middletown unawares, remains in the hands of a group of men—an ex-peanut stand proprietor, an ex-bicycle racer and race promoter, and so on—whose primary concern is making money. (LL267-68)

Do movies show "the ways of the world"? Do they teach sex lessons? Do they lead to promiscuity, "delinquency"? Though wielding a "powerful new education instrument," the theater managers' "primary concern," once again, was "making money."

Like many other Christian denominations, the Assemblies of God proscribed theatergoing and would discipline members who gave in to temptation. Throughout the 1920s the Gospel Publishing House of Springfield's Assemblies of God headquarters printed tracts and journal articles on the subject. Evangel Tract No. 604, "The 'Movies': The Greatest Religious Menace," made "ten indictments against moving pictures as an institution":

First, because of the gigantic financial power that attaches to the business. As a money maker, nothing in history has equaled it. It is not an uncommon thing for producers to spend from one to two million dollars making a single picture....

Second, ... because of the demoralizing effect it is having upon society....

Third, aside from the silly, slapstick comedies that are not even decent caricatures of life, the emphasis is being placed on sex relations....

Fourth, the screen artists are rapidly becoming the ideals for our young people; they are the heroes and heroines of daily conversation. Their beauty, their exquisite clothing, their lax habits and low moral standards are becoming unconsciously appropriated by the plastic minds of American youth....

Fifth, the film world ... teaches a standard of life that will ultimately destroy the home.... Marriage has no sanctity in filmdom. The divorce court ... seems a legitimate avenue of escape....

Sixth, the services of all the great denominations are regularly deserted by the young people crowding into the picture shows; ... large, beautifully decorated theaters fill up and empty from midday to midnight....

Seventh, the moving picture has become the national teacher on all public and religious questions....

Eighth, the thing that suffers more keenly from the "movies" than anything else is Protestantism.... Whenever a Protestant minister figures in a drama it is always a caricature....

Ninth, the moving picture is a persistent determined enemy of the Christian observance of the Lord's Day....

Tenth, the Picture Show is a full graded course of schooling in the technique of crime.... Safe-cracking, pocket-picking, abduction, murder, white slaving—every sort of crime is enacted in the most skillful manner possible, so that all the student need to do is to do as he is taught....

The author attacks from numerous fronts, making several strong claims. While Sunday school attendance was on the decline, the juvenile crime rate and divorce rate were soaring. By the 1920s one in six marriages ended in divorce (Wagner 258). (Like "vacation," the "date," and the "modern woman," "modern divorce" was an invention of the Twenties.)

Having turned its pulpits and private presses against Hollywood, the Christian community's opposition remains part of Springfield's theater history; as such, it needs to be acknowledged and understood. "Practically every movie theater is a school," wrote Evangelist John Carrara in 1922, "and the movie star the teacher of crime and immorality" (81-82). "Study the lives of actresses and actors and you will find that many have been divorced and remarried a number of times.... Is this the kind of thing you want your children to indorse and copy?" (Carrara 84). Springfield's Gospel Publishing House Library regularly lent out its copy of Carrara's *Enemies of Youth;* the book shows considerable use and wear.

For their part, however, Springfield's newspapers (like Middletown's) kept "their hands off the movies" (LL268), refusing to join in the criticism. And no wonder, as "no other agency spends so much in advertising" (Carrara 81). As Lynd and Lynd write, "Save for some efforts among certain of the women's clubs to 'clean up the movies' and the opposition of the Ministerial Association to 'Sunday movies,' Middletown appears content to take the movies at their face value—'a darned good show'—and largely disregard their educational or habit-forming aspects" (LL268-69). Again, the debate over amusements pitted conservative morality and social conscience against *laissez-faire* economics. And economics usually won.

In 1926, Springfield's church groups fought to uphold the Constitutional prohibition of alcohol. In its January 16, 1927 issue the *Springfield Leader* reported on the Victory Day Banquet featuring Dr. A. P. Gouthey, famous evangelist from Seattle, Washington, who was leading the fight nationwide against demon rum. Addressing nearly one hundred supporters, he declared, "What the United States does with the Eighteenth Amendment will largely decide what the world will do with the liquor question." Of course, the "liquor question" raised a far larger list of problems associated with speakeasies and their sensuous pastimes: not just illegal drinking but gambling, jazz, and dancing cheek-to-cheek. (See insert: Springfield and Prohibition.)

In 1916 R. Ritchie Robertson, Springfield's "Star Spangled Scotchman" (G93), became music supervisor for the city's public schools. Among his many accomplishments he remains best known for founding the Springfield Boy Scout Band, which by 1928 had grown to 400 members, making it the "largest Boy Scout Band in the world" (G94). Newsreel footage survives from 1926 celebrating the band's concerts (with violinist David Rubinoff) in Lowe's State Theatre in St. Louis (G114); while there, the band recorded four songs on the Brunswick label. The success of this band and of others that Dr. Robertson organized, including the Abou Ben Adhem Shrine Band, the Frisco Band, and Springfield High School's Kiltie Girls Drum and Bugle Corps (DD92), was moral as much as musical: "Teach your boy to blow a horn and he'll never blow a safe" (G94), Dr. Robertson used to say. (See figure: Kilties on Parade.)

In fact Dr. Robertson sought in classical music and patriotic Sousa marches an antidote to tin pan alley, ragtime, and jazz. Upon assuming his post as Springfield's music supervisor he found "the place saturated with jazz—or I believe it was called ragtime then," Dr. Robertson is said to have quipped, adding, "and I realized immediately that the demand for better music must necessarily be created" (G94). (See insert: "The Demand for Better Music.") The 1920s was, after all, the self-styled "jazz age." What, then, was this "ragtime" that so unsettled Springfield's principal music educator?

In her 1925 essay, "The Great American Art," theater critic Mary Cass Canfield described the defiant, subversive spirit of this new, popular, and quintessentially American musical style:

> Ragtime is the noise that fills an empty room,
> it is the drunkenness of prohibitionists, the

Springfield and Prohibition.
On July 1, 1919 America's Eighteenth Amendment took effect in Missouri, prohibiting the sale and consumption of alcohol. The city had its fiercely devoted temperance workers. Still, like much of the nation, Springfield remained divided. On June 30, when "the last licensed saloon" closed (DD94), "it was estimated that $150,000 was spent in Springfield for liquor that day. Since Prohibition was in force for 14 years, it is unlikely that many of the hoarders made it through the dry spell without illegal provisions" (DD94).

Springfieldians could legally sip Cook's Dry, Bevo, and other near-beers, or they could flout the law. Those who drank did so underground—often literally so, as the area's caves become prime real estate for "moonshine" stills and impromptu speakeasies. An occasional Klan meeting place (nicknamed the Klu Klux Klavern), Percy Cave (later, Fantastic Caverns) north of Springfield was one such speakeasy. Some Springfieldians headed out to Galloway's Half-A-Hill Tea House, a popular night spot featuring both local and nationally-famous dance bands (G122-23). Others headed out to Ozark's Riverside Inn, known for its fried chicken, "bootleg whiskey, slot machines and dancing" (Wingo 8B). Within the city, the current Bodega Bar on Patton Street served as a gin mill: built in 1860 as a livery stable with a doctor's office above it, the historic building has its gin box—still operable today—hidden behind a brick wall.

After ratification of the Twenty-First Amendment in 1933, people popped corks across the Ozarks, having settled the "liquor question" apparently for good.

longing for movement and color of those who sit on packing cases and look in vain for beauty and rhythm up and down Main Street. It is barbarically fierce in its effort to conquer vacuum and the horn of the talking machine is its loud-mouthed interpreter, generously underscoring the violent cheerfulness of its staccato. Barbaric it is and yet subtle, a medley of strange minor gradations running through the major implication of its tone, like the disquiets, the doubts, the melancholy, distressing the American's determined attitude of optimism. (S223)

Lying beneath Canfield's thick pallet of metaphors is a depiction of music that both echoes and rages against the desensitizing, dehumanizing effects of technology and assembly-line labor. Whereas the automobile and, for the most part, the moving picture confirm "Main Street" aspirations, ragtime implicitly mocks the American Dream, rejecting its materialism and naive optimism. "Barbaric it is," writes Canfield: a powerful cultural counterforce, its origins are black, not white. Not the city's formal concert halls but the alley ways and speakeasies echo with its rhythms.

Kilties on Parade.

Such halls as the Shrine Mosque play the "better music," as Dr. Robertson so finely put it. Like its sister jazz, it is an "art with Dionysian frenzy" (S226), as Canfield notes: "The escape of Everyman," jazz plays, rather, "on a blazing stage, full of shapes acrobatically dancing to the exact beat of drums and the seductively insincere moan of saxophones" (S226-27).

Enervated by the new music, the 1920s dance halls (both licensed and illicit) threatened scandal to the town's moral leadership. Yet Springfield would not match Joplin's efforts to legislate against musical immorality. In July 1924, Joplin's city council passed an ordinance prohibiting "cheek to cheek dancing, extreme sidestepping, whirling, dipping, dog walking, shuffling, toddling, Texas tommying, the Chicago hop and walk, the cake-eater or Flapper hop and stiff-arm dancing," adding that "hands must be kept above the waist line" (G93). More likely, Springfield's response mirrored that of Middletown:

> In connection with the moral protest against dancing and the local agitation for stricter regulation of public dance halls, an interesting sidelight is thrown upon the complex nature of such a "social problem" and the piecemeal methods by which people are wont to attack it; although most people try to forbid their children's attending the two public dance resorts outside town because of alleged "immoral conditions," the owner of one of these resorts is a member of the leading civic club whose slogan is "service" and his resort advertised a Sunday night dance with a picture of a partly clad female dancer and the headline, "Plenty Hot!" (LL401)

Here as elsewhere in the urban entertainment industry, business and morality agreed to an uneasy truce.

We have already mentioned a crucial aspect of Springfield's 1920s entertainment industry, one that, while not a technology in itself, rested upon improved roads and the proliferation of automobiles: we refer to the development of Ozarks tourism, in which the city's Chamber of Commerce played a major role. (See figure: "Just Ask Springfield Mo.") Let's end with this theme, as it raises the question of Springfield's corporate identity, one both shaken and subtly reshaped by the Roaring Twenties.

While the 1920s saw a steady stream of inventions enter the household—toasters, vacuum cleaners, refrigerators, electric washing machines and electric irons, to name several—the increased accessibility of the automobile, the moving picture, and the radio changed the ways urban America spent its leisure hours. (See insert: Radio.) Along with "national advertising, syndicated

"The Demand for Better Music." In the December 23, 1924 *Springfield Republican* Dr. Robertson outlined his classically-based music curriculum, confident that it would "affect thousands in the state for years to come, or until the course is amended, if at all." Back then, music education fostered citizenship, civic pride—and a bit of tourism. The city had its own music stores printing their own sheet music, and songs proliferated in praise of Springfield and the Ozarks: "That Ozark Smile" (1920), "Taneycomo" (1922), "The Ozarks are Calling You" (1926), and "My Ozarks" (ca. 1929) can be found among local titles. (See figure: "The Ozarks Are Calling You.") The Chamber of Commerce got into the musical tourist business as well, publishing sheet music for its booster song, "Springfield We are Proud of You" (1922) and for "Everybody's Settin' Jake in Springfield" (ca.1925) (G93-98).

Actually, the Chamber of Commerce offered civics lessons to students directly. In the 1926 *Résumé*, the yearbook of Springfield High School, the Chamber printed its own sort of city-wide pledge of allegiance:

SPRINGFIELD IS MY HOME!

I will be loyal to my Home City — Springfield!

I will support my home city's institutions — its churches, schools, and other organizations for the betterment and welfare of Springfield.

I will support the merchant and professional men of my home city — knowing they are loyal supporters of all that is for the good of Springfield.

I will support the labor of my home city — by advocating the use of "Made in Springfield" products — knowing that by doing so we can increase the payrolls of Springfield....

I will always speak well of my Home City.

THE TRUE CITIZEN.

"The Ozarks are Calling You."

"Just Ask Springfield Mo."

that society is interested in it," be it from "New York, Chicago, Washington or wherever the social centers from which it emanates may be located." Could 1920s Springfield offer the benefits of "big city" life along with down-home Ozarks-country culture? Would the city ground its corporate identity on regional or, rather, on national aspirations and practices? One could, doubtless, trace the development of today's entertainment industry through the Ozarks lakes and hills to the country music Jubilee; certainly the seeds of today's Ozarks-Branson tourism were sown in the 1920s.

But the history of the Gillioz only rarely detours through the Ozarks countryside. Wedded to Springfield's commercial downtown and Route 66, it is specifically an urban history. Our point is simple. Before fashioning its regional tourist identity as "Heart of the Ozarks," Springfield had first to grow up as a city. Though true to its cultural, historic, geographic origins, today's tourist-centered image remains largely nostalgic, a reminiscing (and, in its more Bransonesque effects, a stylized dramatization) of bygone days before urbanization. The Gillioz contributed to Springfield's citifying, reflecting the national, urban character of its entertainments. And these entertainments began with vaudeville, the subject of our next chapter.

newspapers, and other means of large-scale diffusion" (LL271), these technologies served as so many "means of standardizing ... habits" (LL271): in what it wanted, how it thought, and how it spent its money, Springfield came to look pretty much like the rest of Middle America. Even as it sought to invent and (through tourism) to exploit its quasi-rural identity as Queen City of the Ozarks, the technologies of leisure drove Springfield toward greater urbanity, toward more "citified" and fashionable ways of entertaining its citizens and visitors.

New York, Chicago, and Washington were its fashion role models. The June 1, 1902 *Springfield Leader-Democrat* declared as much when reporting on—of all things—the introduction of ping pong: "Springfield is a town always ready to follow a fad as soon as the mandate comes forth

Radio. As Ozarks music historian Wayne Glenn writes, "Radio went from an experimental novelty found in virtually no homes in 1920 to being a million dollar industry with many Ozarks homes having some type of radio receiver as 1929 ended" (G123). Statistics from 1920s Middletown bear him out. "Though less widely diffused as yet than automobile owning or movie attendance," the radio, too, offered a new entertainment technology that was "rapidly crowding its way in among the necessities in the family standard of living" (LL269). As Lynd and Lynd note, "not the least remarkable feature of this new invention is its accessibility.... With but little equipment one can call the life of the rest of the world from the air, and this equipment can be purchased piecemeal at the ten-cent store" (LL269).

In 1926 there were as yet no radio stations in Springfield. WAIA, a low-wattage experimental station, had ceased broadcasting from Heer's Department Store the year before. Major stations in the Ozarks included "KUOA (begun 1922) in Siloam Springs, Arkansas, and WMBH (begun 1927) in Joplin" (G123). Broadcasting from St. Joseph in 1924, Ralph Foster's KGBX Radio would not move to Springfield until 1932 (a move financed by Springfield entrepreneur Lester E. Cox). A second big commercial station, KWTO (also partially owned and managed by Ralph Foster) began broadcasting in 1933 (G131). Prior to World War II, Springfield remained an importer of nationally-broadcast entertainment. Its first major export was the 1940s KWTO radio show, "Korn's-A-Krackin,'" which "was the first regularly broadcast network music show of its type to come from the Ozarks. It brought much attention to the Ozarks as millions heard it on the nationwide Mutual Broadcast System" (G261).

4. Vaudeville!

City man: My friend has been elected mayor.
Country man: Honestly?
City man: What does that matter? ...

Dummy: My father killed a hundred men in the war.
Ventriloquist: What was he? A Gunner?
Dummy: Nope, a cook....

Young man: I want to ask for the hand of your daughter
in marriage.
Old man: You're an idiot!
Young man: I know it. But I didn't suppose you'd object
to another one in the family....
—*The New Vaudeville Joke Book* (1907)

Singers, dancers, skaters, magicians, mimes, mind readers, clowns, comedians, contortionists, acrobats, accordionists, yodelers, ukulele players, tambourine jugglers, boomerang throwers, bird callers, animal acts, billiard acts, electrical acts, novelty ladder acts; some strange, many familiar; some famous, many small-time: all passed through Springfield, booked by one or another of the nation's powerful vaudeville circuits. Will Rogers played the city twice, in "a roping-and-riding" contest in 1899 (Ketchum 61) and with Lucille Mulhall's cowboy troupe in 1900 (Ketchum 70). In August and September of 1908 Lon Chaney played at Doling Park, receiving a handsome $45 per week. Performers at the Jefferson included "Marilyn Miller, who later became a Ziegfeld Follies star; John Barrymore, who went from vaudeville to legitimate theater; Sophie Tucker, who sang here; and a young Joan Crawford under her own name of Lucille LeSeur, who danced in a chorus" (Moser "Springfield's" 39).

When the Jefferson opened its doors on September 28, 1911, its "two-a-day" playbill featured "Advanced Vaudeville." After their overture, the Jefferson Theatre Orchestra accompanied Lee Tung Foo, "Original Chinese Baritone." He was followed by the Romana Brothers, "The World's Greatest Exponents of Physical Culture and Grecian Art" (weight lifters, in other words), who were followed by John West and his "Singing Wolf." A "Character Singer," Flo Collier performed next, followed by the Minstrel Four, "Late Headliners" on the Interstate Circuit. The show ended with Revell and Derry, "Equilibrists" (that is, tightrope walkers). "Photoplays"

were interspersed among the live acts. Quite a bill for one evening, and the theater promised a "Complete Change of Program" each Thursday and Sunday.

The Jefferson quickly became the king of local vaudeville houses, inspiring an intense competition. And yet, the November 22, 1914 *Springfield Leader* reported consecutive years of losses for virtually all the town's theaters. "The Jefferson theater was opened," the *Leader* noted, "and in a short time became a popular amusement center. One night a crowd was turned away. Within a short time there appeared other vaudeville houses. The Landers management gave the new program a trial. Then came disaster to the various projects, and all were threatened with severe losses if not complete ruin." The *Leader* article elaborates:

> Recalling the uncertainties of theatrical ventures in Springfield, the second unfortunate cessation of activities at the Hippodrome theater in the big new Convention Hall has brought to the attention of many Springfield businessmen the fact that during the past few years thousands of dollars, many small fortunes, have been spent on an elusive and deceptive chase of big fortunes which somehow disappeared before the unappreciative public learned what efforts were being put forth in their behalf and for their entertainment.
>
> It has been conservatively estimated that in the past three or four years $50,000 has been expended by theater owners and theatrical syndicates in ventures here that consumed all, or

White City Park.

practically all that was put into the enterprises. Much of the loss has been since 1911, when the motion picture and vaudeville show house began to play important parts in the entertainment of Springfield theatergoers.

In addition to the Hippodrome's failure, the article cited losses for the Lyric, the Grand, the Delmar Garden, and White City, along with the recent burnings of the Perkins Grand Opera and the Baldwin (which their owners refused to rebuild). (See figure: White City Park.) In one respect the losses reflected a simple glutting of the local market: with so many theaters in competition, none could thrive. Yet the deeper cause wasn't competition between houses but between technologies.

On September 4, 1905, the day of its gala opening, the Star Theatre showed the city's first motion pictures (Moser, "Springfield's" 38). The following morning the *Springfield Leader* applauded the theater's "high class vaudeville performance," only briefly mentioning the pictures: "The kinodrome presented 'The Old Maid and the Fortune Teller,' and 'The Great Mine Explosion.' The scenes in the latter particularly were very realistic, and true to mining." The Star's advertisements for the rest of the week reflected a similar nonchalance, listing the kinodrome scenes after the headlining vaudeville. On September 10, the *Leader* announced that "'The Lucky Kitten' and 'The Kleptomaniac,' two new scenes will be presented by the kinodrome" the following Friday for "ladies souvenir day," but the Star's own advertisements

Amateur Orchestra on the Gillioz Stage.

failed to tout the new technology. In fact, the business at such theaters dropped off through 1906, given the poor quality of these early "photoplays." And yet, as movies gained in quality they gained in local popularity. By 1909 nine theaters were showing motion pictures in Springfield (Moser "Springfield's" 39).

In his 1912 essay, "Marvels of the Future," actor's agent and theater critic Robert Grau warned colleagues that "a great menace to the old-time stage and its people" was "looming up on the horizon," the "so-called 'talking picture.' ... Already in London and Paris the talking pictures are a craze" (Stein 343-344). Ever advancing in technology, the movies proved no mere fad, though theater managers "had for a while consoled themselves with the hope that, like other crazes and fads, the vogue of photoplays would be short" (Stein 344). "On the contrary," Grau predicts, "the next two years should record the zenith of achievement in this most lucrative field of public entertaining" (Stein 344). A mere three years later, *Theater Magazine* critic Harold Edwards described the motion picture as "the snowball of the amusement world, rolling over the country and growing bigger and bigger as it annexes theaters, managers, actors and authors" (Stein 340). "Do motion pictures harm children?" "They do if their parents are in vaudeville." So goes the old stage joke.

As McLean notes, "the motion pictures ... did not offer a severe threat in the early days because they could be included within the vaudeville performance itself. But in the Twenties more and more of the smaller or local theaters, squeezed by the cost of 'live' entertainment, resorted to large amounts of film presentation" (M4). Certainly the Gillioz followed this trend: with its October 9, 1927 announcement of "Better Pictures Month," the theater had effectively thrown in vaudeville's towel. In so doing, the Gillioz was anticipating its local rivals. On August 11, 1929, the *Springfield Leader* hinted that "stage vaudeville" had come to an end:

> As the end of the hot summer season comes into view, managers of Springfield theaters are confronted with a rather large problem whether or not to start in the fall with stage vaudeville. The feeling in general, they say, is that stage vaudeville is passé, that screen "shorts" have definitely taken the place of the legitimate stage shows and that it would be useless to attempt a comeback for vaudeville.

Still, in 1926 (the year of the Gillioz opening), vaudeville continued to haunt the nation's stages much like a ghost unaware that it had died. As McLean writes,

> Since 1926 the multimillion dollar circuits had been wobbling, ducking the economic punches of the radio and record companies and the knockout blows of motion pictures. Less than a hundred theaters throughout the country were booking any vaudeville acts at all, and only a dozen of these could be considered "big time." During 1927-1928 the major circuits sold out to the financial syndicates already in control of much radio and record production. The mammoth RKO (Radio-Keith-Orpheum) made gestures toward placing vaudeville once more on its feet, but only the well-established name acts were able to survive.... *Variety* reported that "Vaudeville in 1930 stood motionless on a treadmill that moved backward." ... In 1931 only 675 vaudeville acts were to find a full week of work. (M211)

In the April 1939 issue of *Billboard,* a symposium of newspaper writers responded to the proposition that "for the past ten to fifteen years the favorite subject of show people seems to have been the decline ... of vaudeville. To this day few people agree to whether vaudeville is dead or not" (S247). To other critics' expressions of muted hope, Brooks Atkinson's response proved as simple as true: "On the whole, there is nothing wrong with vaudeville except that it is dead" (S248).

The story just told implies that the Gillioz booked live acts for the first year of its operation and then switched exclusively to film. Nothing could be further from the truth. Though films remained its staple fare, live interludes continued through the early 1950s. Until then, a person visiting the Gillioz could expect the show to open with a rousing rendition of the Star Spangled Banner, played on the Wurlitzer, followed by a song or two from the singing organist or some other local talent; sing-a-longs and other means of audience participation would be encouraged. Child beauty contests, singing contests, swimsuit contests, dance contests abounded. Instead of bringing in outside stars, the Gillioz would claim to be discovering them among its audiences. The difference between the theater's original live-stage ambitions and its actual stage offerings lay, simply, in the price tag: refusing to hire large-scale union acts and orchestras, the theater management turned instead to the city's own local, amateur talent. Though the sheer range and quality of professional variety-vaudeville entertainment would be sacrificed, the theater's live acts would gain from their intimacy with the local audience: indeed they *belonged* to the audience and, in this respect, so did the Gillioz stage. (See figure: Amateur Orchestra on the Gillioz Stage.) The following paragraphs highlight some of the shows to which Gillioz patrons were treated.

∾ ∾

On February 19, 1927, a shopper walking out of Netter's Department Store might see a line forming to her left. On a whim she might reach into her pocket and, finding an extra thirty cents, join the line to take in a show. After all, the morning paper announced that this would be her last chance to see five "big time acts" from the Pantages Vaudeville circuit, headlined by "the original

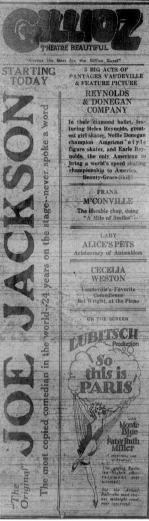

Joe Jackson.

Buster Keaton.

nationally as "the Aristocracy of American Animal Acts," Lady Alice's Pets—a troupe of trained rats that performed with cats, dogs, and pigeons. When the live show ended, the film began: *So This Is Paris*, "a romantic farce about marital infidelity in the City of Love," starring Monte Blue, Patsy Ruth Miller, and Myrna Loy. From comic cycling to roller skating to trained rats to Paris: thirty cents bought our shopper much more than a movie ticket. But she had come to expect such variety: "Always the Best for the Gillioz Guest," ran the theater's motto.

The next day's show touted two acts of "Coast to Coast Vaudeville." The Damaroff Girl Revue (a popular dance chorus line) opened, followed by the novelty act, Princess Elona—a full-blooded Yaqui Indian who sang and "performed native dances in true Indian style." Yet the newspaper's playbill ad featured not the vaudeville but Buster Keaton's silent-film comedy, *The General*. (See figure: Buster Keaton.) "He's here in town tomorrow!" read the *Daily News* ad, as if he were performing in person as part of the vaudeville. To the right of his Hollywood caricature-portrait the come-on read,

That face!
Them eyes!
That look!
Ho! Ho!
Ha! Ha!
Wow! Help!
It's the funniest sight in town.

"The General" brings Buster Keaton in the biggest laugh and thrill show he ever made. Come ride with him, shake and quake with the world's famous "Frozen Face" Fun-Maker! And don't forget—Ron Baggott, "Wizard of the Wurlitzer" making Buster do everything but talk!!

The ad shrewdly acknowledged the live accompaniment, since the organist that evening was none other than Renaldo "Ron" Baggott, an organ-virtuoso who would become part of Seattle's famous "Ron & Don Duo." (It seems that Glenn Stambach, the theater's original "Singing Organist," had yielded the keyboard. Over the years numerous others would follow.)

Baggott, by the way, was "big" enough to be featured on the January 2, 1927 playbill performing "Paul Whiteman's Original Symphonic-Jazz Arrangement of 'Waters of Minnetonka." He would share the stage with Tom Brown and the "original" Six Brown Brothers, who performed with an "Augmented Band of 14 Artists." But neither Baggott nor the Brown Brothers were quite "big"

Joe Jackson," the "Most Copied Comedian in the World." Having toured America and Europe, the "tramp cyclist" Jackson was indeed a major act, one of the biggest to play Springfield. A hobo pantomime (he never spoke a word on stage), Jackson rode his rickety bike, gesturing to his audience for help as it fell to pieces. (In 1942 Jackson died of a heart attack following a curtain call at New York's Roxy Theater. Lying in the wings within earshot of his fans, his dying words—his first uttered on stage—were, "They're still applauding!") (See figure: Joe Jackson.)

Joe Jackson's boss, circuit owner Alexander Pantages, was equally famous and far richer, having built theaters throughout the United States and Canada. His vaudeville circuit reached its height in the mid-1920s, dominating much of the live-variety scene (just before the Crash in 1929, RKO bought out the Pantages circuit for $27,000,000). Other acts that evening included Frank McConville, "the likeable chap doing 'A Mile of Smiles'"; Reynolds & Donegan (that is, Maude Reynolds and Helen Donegan, the "World's Greatest Skating Artists") performing their "diamond ballet"; Cecilia Weston, "Vaudeville's Favorite Comedienne"; and, billed

The Circus!

enough to headline over the evening's featured movie, John Gilbert's *Bardelys the Magnificent,* "Hailed as the Greatest Screen Romance in Years!"

It would be hard to top the playbill for February 20, 1927, though several earlier productions had exceeded it in sheer expense. Performing on January 27, the Watson Sisters lived up to the Gillioz Theatre's ritz. A song and comedy team, the Watsons were "known throughout the world as the highest salaried sister team in vaudeville." Not surprisingly, the morning's *Leader* tucked an announcement in at the bottom of its playbill: "Due to the large salary of the Watson Sisters, we are forced to deviate from our usual policy of five acts, and present four this week with the feature picture." And the February 10 production again raised the ante. As the day's *Leader* declared, "This show, headed by Frank Van Hoven, is by far the most costly road show ever played in Springfield. It will be presented with our regular feature picture at no advance in prices. 'Always the Best for the Gillioz Guest.'" One wonders what props Van Hoven used, as he was billed nationally as "the dippy mad magician who makes ice."

Again offering five "Big Pantages Acts" and a feature picture, the April 8, 1927 show was perhaps the theater's most ambitious. Headlining was "International Star" Francis Renault, the "Original Slave of Fashion, Formerly Featured in the New York Winter Garden ... the Ziegfield Follies and Alhambra, Paris," with "$50,000 Worth of

Wardrobe." A "delineator of feminine types" (in modern parlance, a female impersonator), Renault put on a runway revue in which he himself modeled the latest women's fashions. The second act, Lester and Irving's "Superlative Slow Motion," was a slapstick performed in slow-mo. Little Cecil was the day's third novelty act, billed as the "World's Youngest Mind Reader." Fourth on the bill were Mack and Tempest performing the comedy playlet, "Once But Not Twice." The fifth act featured "A Beautiful Presentation of Song, Dance, and Music" by the Busch Sisters, with Harry Chalapin and Mogiloff's Orchestra. Regularly performing with the nationally-renowned Busch Sisters, Mogiloff's was a Russian balalaika band. Finally, "On the Screen" was shown *A Little Journey,* starring William Haines and Claire Windsor: "Here's a surprise picture for you—3,000 miles of love and laughter—a thrill and a roar for every mile. Unlimited fun on the Overland Limited." Ensconced in the Pantages circuit, the Gillioz was working like a big-time, big-city theater whose entertainment was non-stop and its vaudeville performed "three-a-day": pictures showed at 1:00, 4:15, 5:30, 8:15, and 10:15, vaudeville at 2:50, 6:30, and 9:05.

The July 13, 1927 *Daily News* advertised "America's Greatest Stage Circus / 10 Big Acts" on the Gillioz stage. There was Bee Ho Gray & Co. giving a "roping and whip cracking exhibition" and Miss Ada Somerville with "her dancing pony, 'Onions.'" There were the Three Kaswell Sisters—"a thrilling ring, web and trapeze act"—and Mike the Monk, "a tiny little star of the big show." There were "Clowns! Clowns! Clowns!" and "Moments of song and dance!" There was "the amazing knife thrower—human lives depending on the twist of the wrist!" There was a bucking mule and riders—"the funniest thing you ever saw!" There was "Happiness for youngsters and oldsters.... You'll laugh from start to finish!" And all "Just like under the canvas top—only inside a theater—cool and comfortable!" (See figure: The Circus!)

✂ ✂

The above lets us sample the live acts featured its first year, when the Gillioz operated full-steam as a "combination" theater. Perhaps cloyed by the continuous richness of fare, the audiences inevitably slacked off. Following the theater's retreat from variety-vaudeville, the Gillioz management tried numerous come-ons to retrieve audiences, most aimed at housewives and children.

Through the week of November 14, 1927, women were invited to attend "five remarkable lectures" by *"Mm. Chernoff, the International Authority* and Writer on Beauty-Charm and Health Culture":

> Beauty is only the card of entre', the creator of first impression. It attracts but it cannot hold... . By applied knowledge and proper care any woman can become beautiful. By the science of *Well Being* any woman can develop a charming personality. To acquire this knowledge you have but to hear this noted authority....

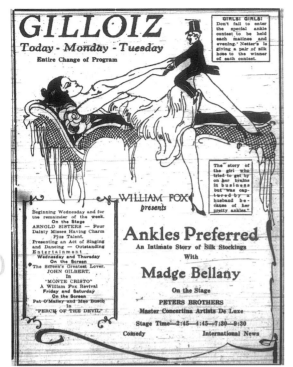

Ankles Preferred.

Having learned beauty's secrets, the city's women would grace the stage in a variety of amateur swimsuit and talent contests. On June 26, 1927 (while the theater was still showing vaudeville), the Gillioz announced its "special ankle contest," held "each matinee and evening" during the run of *Ankles Preferred*—"an intimate story of silk stockings," starring Madge Bellamy. Audiences clapped for the most attractive pair of ankles and the winner received a pair of silk hose from Netter's next door—a shrewd wedding of beauty and business. (See figure: *Ankles Preferred.*) From July 17 to July 20, 1927, Catherine Beal—recently crowned Miss Springfield—appeared on stage. (See figure: "Meet 'Miss Springfield.'") On July 20, Miss Beal shared the spotlight with dancers entered in the theater's "Black Bottom Contest," one of several dance contests held that year.

Co-sponsored by the *Springfield Press,* a "Pageant of Glorious Girlhood" took place from May 26 to May 30, 1931. (See figure: "Pageant of Glorious Girlhood.") The *Press* ad for May 26 calls it "Springfield's First Beauty Pageant." More accurately, it was the city's first participation in the "International Pageant of Pulchritude" (a rival to Atlantic City's Miss America Pageant) held annually in Galveston, Texas, through the 1920s and 1930s. Here, too, beauty allied itself with local business, as each contestant represented one of the newspaper's advertisers. "Springfieldians never before have seen as fine a group of young women as were presented Tuesday night on the stage of the Fox-Gillioz Theatre," the *Press* reported. (See figure: "Who Will Be Miss Springfield?") (By this date the Gillioz had joined the Fox Midwest chain: but unlike the renamed Fox-Electric, the Gillioz name change didn't stick.) Helen Bennett, a "robust athletic type of beauty" with "lustrous brown hair, brown eyes and pretty teeth," won the coveted title.

Having attracted their men through such contests, Springfield's women would next be taught how to keep them. An ad in the December 5, 1934 *Daily News* read,

Some of the highlights of her teachings are—How to remove wrinkles, tighten flabby skin, reduce without strenuous exercise—or dieting; overcome nervousness, increase your vitality, acquire poise and charm. Personal questions answered at the end of each lecture. Don't miss a single one!

Though the *Daily News* ad declared "Everyone Welcome," the fifth lecture was "For Women only: Intimate Discussion." Hmm.

GILLIOZ
SPECIAL!
Ladies Only Matinees!
Now & Tomorrow
Dr. Zomar at 3 P. M. Only

Dr. Karl Zomar
PSYCHOLOGIST
Will Answer All Questions
And Lecture On
"Successful Marriage"

20¢ All Seats to 6 P.M.

With "Successful Marriage" came children, and those who inherited their mothers' talents would take the stage, in turn. The annual Christmas pageants were custom-made for the kiddies. One particular flier

"Meet 'Miss Springfield.'"

"Pageant of Glorious Girlhood."

announced a "Gala Yuletide Stage Show" for December 12 and 13, 1928:

ANNA LOUIS HORN BOSTEL
Presents
*"Kris Kringle
Toyland Review"*

Cast of 100 of Springfield's
Cleverest Youngsters
with
Wally Stoeffler And His
Santa Claus Orchestra

Inviting the city's "Cleverest Youngsters" on stage, such

"Who Will Be Miss Springfield?"

shows packed the house with proud grandparents. On October 31, 1931, Anna Bostel and Wally Stoeffler again joined forces in a children's production, the "Hallowe'en Goblin Frolic." Featuring "Sixty-five of Springfield's Most Talented Kiddies in a Colorful Musical Dance Revue," the show made use of a "New and Spectacular Lighting Effect—STROBELITE."

If the Gillioz stage belonged to the city's younger amateurs, Springfield's matrons owned the mezzanine, where afternoon bridge parties were served free coffee and the Sorosis Club held its spring flower shows. And we should add that the amateur stage met with some jealousy. On December 5, 1934 (the same day that Dr. Zomar lectured on "Successful Marriage"), the *Daily News* reported that "Presentation of two comedy skits by the Springfield Little Theater group, scheduled to be given on the stage of the Gillioz theater tonight and tomorrow night, has been canceled." Vogel Gettier, manager of the theater, blamed the local union:

> "The musicians informed me," said Mr. Gettier, "that unless there were a 7-piece union orchestra in the pit, the show could not go on. Since the two skits do not require music—even by a pianist—we did not feel that an orchestra was needed....
>
> "The stage show planned was strictly an amateur performance by a group of young people who are trying to accomplish something in dramatics and I don't see any reason why the union musicians should stand in their way...."

Here, too, the curtain would have risen to an amateur production. But note the union's strength (which could dictate terms of any stage performance) and the implicit antagonism between amateur and professional: during the Depression, the amateur stage took bread off a union family's table, and neither management nor the union was keen on losing revenue. Citizens complained over the next several days, but the union held firm.

Through the 1940s the Gillioz stage enjoyed a renascence of live entertainment, though again on a smaller scale than that of the old variety-vaudeville. Along with news reels and cartoons, the afternoon "Gillioz Hour" would feature contests and quiz shows, organ concerts and an occasional dance band or vocal group. In fine civic fashion, the Gillioz joined with the Fox-Electric in hosting a presidential "Straw Vote Day." As both theaters' *Daily News* ads for October 26, 1940 read, "Be here to mark your ballot and to hear the issues debated by local people!" The "Gillioz Hour" for June

Clinton at the Wurlitzer.

La Zingara.

5, 1941 featured Freddie Martin and His Orchestra; the "Gillioz Hour" for July 4 featured Ted Husing's "Acrobatic Aces," Pete Smith's "Cuban Rhythm," and Marie Greene and Her Orchestra.

In 1944 "The Gillioz Organ Song Fest," billed as *"The Show That Stars Springfield!"* became part of the theater program. An "Internationally Famous Organist ... Formerly at the Paramount, Los Angeles," British-born Arthur Clinton led audiences in sing-alongs that evolved into full-blown talent contests. (See figure: Clinton at the Wurlitzer.) Several souvenir programs survive, one describing the "Beauty With A Voice" competition:

> With the idea of furthering music in Springfield ... giving other talented young singers an opportunity to show professionally ... it was decided by Art and the theatre management to hold a contest to be called the "Beauty With A Voice" ... and from more than two score of applicants who auditioned for the opportunity to sing before Gillioz audiences ...15 were selected ... given special training ...and a week's engagement at the Gillioz.
>
> The Gillioz patrons were asked to vote for their favorite ... after the fifteen week period was at an end ... and with nearly 10,000 votes tabulated—Marilyn Brown and Mary May Morgan were given five week contracts to sing with the Gillioz Trio. The next venture at the Gillioz? Art's planning now on giving boys and girls under 12 years of age the opportunity to sing at the the-

atre ... and over the air ... in a new program originating from the Gillioz on Wednesday mornings beginning May 29th for a six week's period!

Time marches on ... and the Gillioz audiences keep singing!

There was one rather ambitious ballet production, apparently a collaboration between professional and amateur dancers: a poster from the 1940s announces the Saroff De Brae Dancers in *La Zingara,* "A Gypsy Ballet," featuring "a Corps de Ballet of 40 Dancers." (Quite a crowd for such a shallow stage!) (See figure: *La Zingara.*)

By 1946 KTTS was broadcasting shows live from the Gillioz. On October 11 the Gillioz touted its "Saturday Morning Kiddies Show!" With doors opening 9:00 a.m. and "all seats 25¢," the theater would likely have been packed with children pulling their parents in tow. And why not? Look at the morning's line up: "30 Minutes of Your Favorite Cartoons," including Bugs Bunny and Little Lulu, the feature film *My Pal, Wolf,* starring the young Sharyn Moffett,

— Plus: —
Kiddies' Amateur
Show Broadcast
Cash Prizes Awarded Weekly.
Broadcast over KTTS
and Heer's Toyland
Quiz Program.

Of course Heer's (the show's radio sponsor) would get in on the program. Christmas was coming and the kids

Bob Barker at the Gillioz.

would be pining over toys in its store windows. (See figure: Bob Barker at the Gillioz.)

Like other theaters after World War II, the Gillioz attracted audiences through give-aways: door prizes, free groceries, gift stamps. "Dish Night" was particularly popular, as patrons received a new piece of tableware each week. There was "Good Cheer Week," when "a free pass will be given to everyone attending who does not receive a smile and a friendly greeting from every theater employee!" Through the mid-1950s, special events continued to bring the Gillioz stage back to life. None was more special, though, than the June 7, 1952 world premiere of *The Winning Team*. "On Stage and In Person," read the newspaper ad, the Gillioz would feature "Ronald Reagan, Star of *The Winning Team*," Gene Nelson, "Warner Brothers Dancing Star of *Starlift*," Virginia Gibson, "Warner Brothers Dancing Star of *About Face*," and Nancy Davis, "Glorious Dramatic Star," along with Mrs. Grover Cleveland Alexander. But such live-stage events, whether professional or amateur, eventually ended. By the 1970s the movie screen had been bolted to the floor and the stage behind it filled with huge speakers and subwoofers, the legacy of Sensaround sound. Sitting in the dusty, silent pit, the organ console was covered by

a tarp. It was only a matter of time before the "Mighty Wurlitzer" was sold off.

But we shouldn't mourn overlong the live stage's fated passing. We have just mentioned *The Winning Team* and it's time that we turn to the Gillioz Theatre's greater claim to fame, its history with movies. Three movies are often mentioned as having premiered at the Gillioz: *Jesse James* (1939), starring Henry Fonda and Tyrone Power, *The Shepherd of the Hills* (1941), starring John Wayne and Harry Carey, and *The Winning Team* (1952), starring Ronald Reagan and Doris Day. Our research tells a different story.

Lights of New York.

5. Lights, Camera, ...

Major Rufus Cobb: [Jesse] was one of the doggonedest,
gawl-dingedest, dad-blamedest buckaroos that ever rode
across these here United States of America!

—*Jesse James* (1939)

Ed Hatch: Hey, anyone in that barn?
Kids: That's not a barn, that's a blacksmith's shop.
Ed Hatch: Oh, is the blacksmith in?
Kids: Yeah. (Shouting) Hey, mom! ...

—*Swing Your Lady* (1939)

Jerry Jones: will you marry me tonight?
Ethel: Well, of course.
Jerry Jones: Wonderful. Congratulations, darling, you're
a war bride. I've just been drafted.

—*This Is the Army* (1943)

The Gillioz Theatre's October 11, 1926 *Souvenir Book* touted coming film attractions. Reginald Denny's *Take it From Me* would be followed by *The Flaming Frontier,* starring the popular cowboy hero, Hoot Gibson. Next would be the M.G.M. "extravaganza," *La Boheme,* starring Lillian Gish, King Vidor and John Gilbert. These would be followed by *The Waning Sex, Poker Faces, The Whole Town Talking,* and *The Old Soak.* In the October 9, 1927 *Leader* the Gillioz management announced its "Greater Movie Season," featuring "a series of as fine pictures as the market affords": *Ben-Hur, Spring Fever, The Coward, The Chinese Parrot, The Bugle Call,* and *The Big Parade.* In November 1927 came "Better Pictures Month," featuring *The Harvester, The Collegians, The Garden of Allah, In Old Kentucky, On Your Toes,* and *Man, Woman, and Sin.* After these came *Annie Laurie, Moment of Temptation, Back to God's Country,....* From this distance, none besides *Ben-Hur* remains memorable. Even the most film-savvy of today's theatergoers is unlikely to have heard, much less have seen, more than two of the above.

But the advent of sound soon rocked the cinema world. In the November 11, 1928 *News and Leader* the Gillioz advertised its "Gala" showing of the gangster melodrama, *Lights of New York,* in "Perfected Vitaphone":

It's Here

Now—Right Now! "Perfected Vitaphone"—No longer the dream of tomorrow—but the reality of today....

The cozy intimacy, friendly hospitality of this theater beautifully combined with its perfect acoustics will bring to you your greatest enjoyment of the new type of entertainment—Motion Pictures that Sing and Talk!

Though claiming that "the Gillioz leads in offering" Springfield's audiences "the pick of the new era entertainment," the theater was just catching up to the Landers, which showed its first Vitaphone film earlier that year. Billed as the "first 100% talking picture," *Lights of New York* showed at the Gillioz, along with two reels of Vitaphone vaudeville. (See figure: *Lights of New York.*)

The year 1928 altered the face of downtown Springfield as marquee after marquee changed names. Of course the silent-film nickelodeons went out of business. The Ritz (on Boonville Avenue) closed, wired up for sound, and reopened as the Royal. The Grand (on the southwest corner of the Square, caddy corner to the Electric) closed, wired up, and reopened as the Iris (renamed the Mozark in 1934). (See figure: Mozark on the Square.) And the Mullikin (also on Boonville) had its gala in 1928, all ready and wired for sound (Moser "Earliest" 34). Keeping up with the cinematic Joneses, the Electric remodeled in 1930: renamed the Fox-Electric, it too featured the new sound equipment.

If Springfield's 1929 audiences were anything like those of Middletown, then the theater business was booming. Due to sound, the nation's movie attendance

Mozark on the Square.

had reached 110 million, twice the attendance in 1927. In its *Leader* ad for January 12, 1929 the Gillioz called itself "Springfield's most popular theatre." There's no reason to doubt it. On April 12 the "General Electric Equipped" Gillioz showed M.G.M.'s first all-talking Movietone sound-on-film musical, *The Broadway Melody*, winner of the first Academy Award for Best Picture. (See figure: *The Broadway Melody.*)

But all this was before Black Tuesday, October 29, 1929, when the Stock Market Crash sent the nation's economy into a decade-long tail spin. By 1932 the Great Depression had pummeled the Ozarks and its theaters. As a brief article in the June 11 *Press* reported, "Springfield's theaters will be reduced to four this weekend with the scheduled closing of the Springfield Paramount and the Landers theaters for the summer." Offering no explanation, the article ended with a little good news: "Three changes a week at the Gillioz, however, will keep Springfield supplied with first-run films of excellent quality." The morning paper offered a bit more detail:

> The Springfield Paramount and Landers theaters ... will close indefinitely Saturday.... Motion picture operators had offered to accept a reduction in wages if given a year's contract but their offer was not accepted on those terms. No date for opening of the theaters has been set but it is understood that they will be closed for the summer at least.

Nothing definite has been decided regarding closing of the Fox-Plaza theater, part of the Fox chain.... Notices have been given and the theater is operating on a week-to-week basis waiting to determine if business conditions will change.... Fox theaters have had no dispute with motion picture operators regarding wages.

Apparently the Gillioz was turning a profit while other theaters fought to survive. The Jefferson, too, fell victim to the sad economy, closing its doors until 1948 (Marymount 2D).

Paradoxically, America's Great Depression was Hollywood's Golden Age. Film technology continued its advances, culminating in "three-strip" Technicolor. Assuming one could afford a ticket, the movies now lent color to an otherwise hard life. On January 16, 1936 the animated short film, *Time for Love* showed at the Gillioz; it was likely the first Technicolor film to play at the Theatre Beautiful. *The Trail of the Lonesome Pine* (the first Technicolor film shot on location, starring Sylvia Sydney and Fred MacMurray) showed on April 20; on October 10 *Ramona* (starring Loretta Young and Don Ameche) showed in "Perfected" Technicolor. *Snow White and the Seven Dwarfs* (Disney's first full-length color cartoon, taking three years and $1,500,000 to make) showed on March 10, 1938, offering Springfieldians "A Miracle Show Whose Every Magic Minute is a Joy Forever!"

Yet 1938 was memorable for more than *Snow White*

The Broadway Melody.

and its "Multiplane Technicolor." More importantly, the Gillioz hosted its first world premiere. Once again the stage would come alive, and not with amateur talent.

≈ ≈

Of all Ozarkers that have achieved fame in vaudeville and film, the Weaver family remains the region's most influential and culturally important. Leon "Abner" Weaver, master of the "musical saw" and other home-made instruments, Frank "Cicero" Weaver (who never spoke but, like a hillbilly Harpo Marx, gesticulated on stage), and the loud, uncouth June "Elviry" Weaver played the Landers but never the Gillioz. (See figure: The Weaver Brothers and Elviry.) In an appreciative biography, Reta Spears-Stewart highlights the family's success:

> The family show was unique in its down-home flavor and homemade musical instruments. But if that had been all there was the Weaver Brothers and Elviry would have quickly faded from the scene. Instead, they became an American institution and a template for a thousand other rural acts. They remained a top-billed entertainment organization for nearly forty years.
>
> The Weaver Brothers and Elviry received such tributes as being "held over" at New York's Palace Theatre and doing command performances all over Europe. Besides vaudeville and road shows, the constantly growing troupe developed a popular weekly radio program broadcast from Springfield on radio station KWTO.
>
> Then, during World War II, they went on to "dabble" in the production of a dozen or

so movies, featuring the likes of Humphrey Bogart, Penny Singleton, Roy Rogers, Alan Ladd, Roy Acuff, Frankie Darrow, Ann Jeffries—and a first movie for a young actor named Ronald Reagan. (Spears-Stewart, "Weavers" 2: 62)

Again, the Weavers never played the Theatre Beautiful. (See insert: The Weavers and the Gillioz.) Yet the above reference to movies and "a young actor named Ronald Reagan" marks an important milestone for the Gillioz: its premiere showing of *Swing Your Lady,* starring Humphrey Bogart, Penny Singleton, Nat Pendleton, Louise Fazenda, … and the Weaver Brothers and Elviry.

The premiere took place on January 14, 1938. With typical bravado the morning's newspaper ad proclaimed it "The Most Auspicious Theatrical Event Ever Staged in Springfield! Lights! Celebrities! Glamour! Mr. and Mrs. Frank Weaver (Cicero and Elviry) Guests of the Theater!" A hillbilly musical comedy, *Swing Your Lady* tells the story of a broke fight manager (Humphrey Bogart) and his dim-witted wrestler (Nat Pendleton), whose car breaks down in a ditch, stranding them in the Ozarks. Helped out by an amazon-woman blacksmith, the manager (impressed by her strength and looking for fast money) promotes a match between the woman and his wrestler, who proceeds to fall head-over-heels in love with her and refuses to fight—that is, until her dumb boyfriend shows up. The Weaver Brothers and Elviry essentially play themselves, in part redeeming the movie's thin plot through their own folksy charm. The young Ronald Reagan had a small role as sportscaster (it was his third film appearance). Bogart was of course

The Weavers and the Gillioz. *Though not as live performers, members of the Weaver clan were often seen among the Gillioz Theatre's audiences. Actually, at least one Weaver—Charles, the brother of Frank and Leon—worked for a time in the Gillioz management. Charles had performed with his brothers in their early medicine shows and worked as a manager for the Landers before being lured away by the new Gillioz to serve as its first stage manager. In 1928, however, he left (perhaps because of the theater's turn from vaudeville) to join his older brothers back on stage when they formed the "Weaver Brothers and Home Folks" show (Spears-Stewart, "Weavers" 5: 32).*

The History Museum for Springfield-Greene County has a "Route Sheet" or itinerary for the 1936 Weaver Brothers and Elviry and Home Folks Show. It shows a packed schedule working the RKO circuit. Circling the United States and Canada, the troupe took weekly "jumps" or train rides for engagements beginning in St. Louis and then working its way east through New York State, back through the Central states and Midwest, across to the Northwest and Canada, down the West Coast, across the Southwest, and ending seven months later in Kansas City. Over twenty-four weeks of travel, the Weavers had a "Total of 26 days open." Grueling! Though their fame (and traveling) was international, the Weavers were never uprooted from the Ozarks. They lived here in style, though, having bought the majestic Heer mansion (built by Charles Heer of Heer's Department Store fame) overlooking the James River between Springfield and Nixa.

The Weaver Brothers and Elviry.

the movie's headliner, though one couldn't tell this from the *Leader* ad, which read "The Weavers Bros and Elviry in 'Swing Your Lady' with Louise Fazenda, Humphrey Bogart, Frank McHugh,...." (See figure: *Swing Your Lady*.)

In the next day's article, "Springfield Stages Movie Premiere—Stars and Everything," the *Leader and Press* gave the event splashy, Hollywood-style coverage, running photos of the stars arriving at the theater. The event was covered by local radio, as well. (See figure: Weavers Arrive at the Gillioz.) As one photo caption read,

A crushing mob of fans started gathering outside the Gillioz theater at 6:30 o'clock last night, to get a glimpse of the Weavers as they arrived for the premiere.... The crowd filled the sidewalk and part of the street in front of the theater, requiring a squad of policemen to hold them back, and even overflowed into the foyer.... In the picture above you see part of the crowd in the foyer and, in the center, Cicero and Elviry as they made their appearance. When they arrived at the

Swing Your Lady.

theater the famous couple paused at the microphone to say a few words to radio listeners before going in to see themselves for the first time on the screen.

After the movie, reporters accompanied the Weavers across the street to the Colonial Hotel, where a reception followed for two hundred guests.

Now, one might expect that the first showing of the first movie ever filmed by the city's most famous family act would get rave local reviews. In fact, the movie flopped in Springfield. The audience took its cues from the Weavers themselves, "who watched the picture with silent interest.... Frank laughed only once during the picture, [and] June's only big laugh came at Frank's expense." What went wrong? In his review, *Leader and Press* reporter Allen Oliver was unabashedly critical on two points. First, the movie failed to exploit the Weavers' full comic talents. Second, it failed in its depiction of Ozarks life and culture:

To view objectively a picture in which you have considerable personal interest is a difficult thing to do, as we discovered last night when we watched "Swing Your Lady," which features the Weaver Brothers and Elviry in their Screen debut.

We don't think we are swayed by prejudice when we say that those sequences in which the Weavers appear were the best sequences in the picture, and that despite the fact that the producers failed to sell the trio to the public as they might have. Maybe that's prejudice also, but it appeared that Warner Brothers realized too late that they had a valuable property, and then didn't know what to do with it....

Like all pictures with an Ozarks background, this one was pretty highly flavored with some one's interpretation of what life is like in the Ozarks, an interpretation that must have come to them in a dream. It couldn't have been the result of experience or observation. The Weavers

attempted to act as technical advisers as well as actors when the picture was being made, but all their arguments couldn't sway a Hollywood producer.

People in other sections of the country, we fear, are going to get the impression that all people do in small towns in the Ozarks is sit on a front porch and play and sing hillbilly songs from morning until night, and when night comes they go to a square dance. All the people who live in the hills will be thought to resemble the characters in the hillbilly cartoons in Esquire, and talk like something between a negro mammy and an Arizona cowboy. It is something of an anomaly that the Weavers' accent, the only genuine Ozarks accent in the picture, sounded somehow out of place and unnatural....

Such a review makes explicit the city's ambivalence toward the Ozarks' hillbilly stereotype. It was okay for the Weavers to exploit the stereotype for comedy (and money). But Springfieldians knew it was a stereotype; the rest of the country, however....

What other premieres did the Theatre Beautiful host? While *Jesse James* is often mentioned as a Gillioz premiere, neither Springfield nor the Gillioz can legitimately lay claim to it. Though the James Brothers belong to Springfield lore, this movie—the first Technicolor western shot on location, costing $25,000 to make—rightfully belongs to Pineville, Missouri, where it was filmed, and to the Orpheum Theatre in Tulsa, Oklahoma, where it premiered January 13, 1939. Yet Springfield and the Frisco did play their own small roles in the filming and the February 4, 1939 Gillioz opening was as lively as a premiere. After all, several individuals involved in the movie were proudly in attendance. (See figure: *Jesse James*.)

The September 11, 1938 *Leader and Press* reported on local Frisco employees who "helped operate the train which Jesse ... robs in the picture ... now being filmed at Pineville." The movie's spin on the James Gang's train-robbing—that they were American western Robin Hoods striking blows against the encroaching railroad and its money-grubbing agents—was perhaps lost on these Frisco railroaders; otherwise, they didn't mind seeing their profession cast among the "bad guys." We should add that Jesse—Tyrone Power, actually—stole

Weavers Arrive at the Gillioz.

EPIC DRAMA OF A LAWLESS AND TURBULENT ERA THAT GAVE THE WORLD ITS MOST FAMOUS OUTLAW!

DARRYL F. ZANUCK'S PRODUCTION OF

THE MOST EXCITING PICTURE YOU HAVE EVER SEEN

JESSE JAMES

In TECHNICOLOR

starring

TYRONE POWER
HENRY FONDA
NANCY KELLY
RANDOLPH SCOTT

and

Henry Hull · Slim Summerville
J. Edward Bromberg · Brian Donlevy
John Carradine · Donald Meek
John Russell · Jane Darwell

Directed by Henry King

A 20th Century-Fox Picture

Hunted Killer!..yet to one he was gentle and brave!

STARTS

TOMORROW!

Doors Open 12:45

Jesse James.

more than train money. He also stole the heart of Mary Jane Smeadley, a local beauty with whom he had a serious if brief affair, bringing her to Hollywood for screen tests. (See figure: Tyrone Power.)

The Shepherd of the Hills cannot be claimed for the Gillioz, either, having officially opened in New York City on July 9, 1941. But, curiously from today's distance, it does not seem that the Ozarks wanted much to do with this "Hollywood version of the book that, next to the Bible, is still the best seller in the Ozarks": so wrote a reporter in the June 8, 1941 *Kansas City Star*. In a photo-essay titled "'Shepherd of the Hills': Hollywood's Version and the Ozarks Reality," the *Star* reporter juxtaposed stills from the upcoming movie with actual photographs of the Ozarks and its people. He then reported the local response: "Residents of the hill country say, after seeing some stills, that the film, made in the San Bernadino Mountains of extreme Southern California, will not be their 'Shepherd of the Hills.'" Evidently Hollywood's tourists and film-makers couldn't see the difference. As the July 29, 1941 *Oakland (CA) Tribune* reported,

> When tourists visit the San Bernadino Mountains in California, apparently the scenic beauty isn't the only lure, for it has been discovered that travelers go many miles out of their way to see the small village and the cabins that were erected for the Paramount technicolor drama, "Shepherd of the Hills." …
>
> Resembling closely the majestic Ozark moun-

tains, … director Henry Hathaway chose the San Bernadino mountains for the filming of this romantic drama.

Beyond geography, the Hollywood version faced problems of characterization, since any depiction of well-known figures fell in danger of caricature. Writing in the July 21, 1941 *Oakland Tribune,* theater critic Wood Soanes acknowledged the problem, though he suggests that this one has been solved:

> Millions of readers have preconceived notions concerning the characters created by Harold Bell Wright for the "Shepherd of the Hills,".… But Director Henry Hathaway knew that none of those readers would disagree with his choice in gruff Harry Carey for the title role.
>
> The casting of the other roles was not so easy. But Hathaway's choice of John Wayne as young Matt, the Ozark mountain boy who has vowed to kill his father, and Betty Fielder as the wild mountain girl, has proven a faithful reflection of Wright's popular characters.

A "faithful reflection," to be sure: adding "color" to Wright's plot, Hollywood's script writers turned the Matthews family into a disagreeable gang of moonshiners. And that's just for starters.

Soanes corrected himself three days later, in the July 24 *Oakland Tribune*. His article, "Ozarks Angry at Film 'Realism': Citizens Object to Dated Conditions Depicted in Harold Bell Wright Tale," notes the uproar Hollywood's *Shepherd* caused in Branson, leading to the movie's public denunciation and even a little picketing:

> If Paramount felt that it was cementing friendship between Hollywood and the Ozark Mountains through the medium of the technicolor "Shepherd of the Hills" it was indulging itself in a typical cinema error of judgment.
>
> The town of Branson, Missouri, is pretty typical of the Ozarks, and the town of Branson is hopping mad. The ire has reached such a peak that after the first showing of the film the enterprising manager of the theater armed himself with a sign reading "Unfair to Local Characters" and proceeded to picket his own house.…
>
> Town sentiment was reflected in the statement of Rev. J. F. Chase … who was among those invited to watch the preview. He said, "I consider 'The Shepherd of the Hills' picture the most deplorable production I have ever seen."

And Branson continued to fight back. In an article, "The Home Folk in Their Own 'Shepherd of the Hills,'" the September 21 *Kansas City Star* reported on a local production: "The Ozarks folk vowed they would 'do it right,'" the *Star* noted. Returning to Wright's own 1912 stage version of his novel, the city produced its own *Shepherd* on its own live stage, using local actors.

By now, surely, the city of Branson has gotten over its anger. With some confidence, though, we can conclude the following. Prior to the development of Branson's own Hollywood-style tourist industry, the Ozarks remained wary of "outside" depictions of the region, its characters and its ways. "Whatever we are," one might imagine an Ozarker saying back then, "we aren't that." (See insert: On Ronald Reagan and Harold Bell Wright.)

The American Film Institute lists the movie's release date as July 9, 1941. This creates a puzzle, though, as *The Shepherd of the Hills* opened at the Gillioz on July 4 and played through July 11. (See figure: *The Shepherd of the Hills*.) Our searches (admittedly incomplete) through national newspaper databases have turned up no earlier showings anywhere. And yet, beyond the daily advertisements, the Springfield newspapers make no mention of the movie or of the crowds' reactions. Though not a full-blown world premiere, could the movie have had a quiet sneak-preview at the Gillioz? We cannot dismiss (or disprove) the possibility.

Strictly speaking, the next movie was not a world

Tyrone Power.

On Ronald Reagan and Harold Bell Wright. The *Kansas City Star* was right in declaring Wright's novel "next to the Bible" in influence upon its Ozarks readership. More than moralizing and sentimental, *The Shepherd of the Hills* is heroic in its characterizations, and we shouldn't blame Hollywood for having tried. After all, Hollywood was in the business of hero-making, of creating film stars whose larger-than-life characterizations preached manliness, "rugged individualism," and spotless virtue to America's youth.

Notably, one particular American-Dream-maker—Ronald Reagan—found his own spiritual role model in the writings of Harold Bell Wright (1872-1944). Writing on White House stationary, President Reagan sent the following letter to Jean Wright, second wife of the novelist's youngest son, Norman Wright:

THE WHITE HOUSE
WASHINGTON

March 13, 1984

Dear Mrs. Wright:

It is true that your father-in-law's book, indeed books, played a definite part in my growing-up years. When I was ten or eleven years old, I picked up Harold Bell Wright's book, *That Printer of Udell's*, which I'd seen my mother reading, and read it from cover to cover. Perhaps I should tell you I became an avid reader at a very early age and had my own card for the Dixon, Illinois Public Library. I made regular use of the card.

That book, *That Printer of Udell's*, had an impact I shall always remember. After reading it and thinking about it for a few days, I went to my mother and told her I wished to be baptized. We attended the Christian Church in Dixon, and I was baptized several days after finishing the book.

The term, "role model," was not a familiar term in that time and place. But I realize I found a role model in that travelling printer whom Harold Bell Wright had brought to life. He set me on a course I've tried to follow even to this day. I shall always be grateful.

Sincerely,
Ronald Reagan

"A sermonic melodrama" (Chudleigh), *That Printer of Udell's* (1903) was Wright's first novel, soon to be followed by his second and best-selling *Shepherd of the Hills* (1907). We have no reason to doubt Reagan's sincerity: our 40th President was thus "saved" through an Ozarks preacher-turned-novelist's literary characterizations.

The Shepherd of the Hills.

premiere, either. But the patriotic fanfare surrounding the September 23, 1943 "'First Nighter' Premiere" of *This Is The Army* made it one of Springfield's and the Gillioz Theatre's more memorable movie events. In his *All Movie Guide,* Hal Erickson gives the plot:

> The splashy, star-studded *This Is The Army* is based on the Irving Berlin Broadway musical of the same name, which in turn was a reworking of Berlin's WW1 "barracks musical" *Yip Yip Yaphank.* In both instances, the cast was largely composed of genuine servicemen, many of them either recently returned from fighting or on the verge of heading off to war. The Hollywood-imposed storyline concerns Jerry Jones (George Murphy), a member of the original 1918 *Yip Yip Yaphank* cast. His showbiz career curtailed by a leg injury, Jerry becomes a producer during the postwar era. When the US enters WW2, Jerry gathers together several other cast members from the 1918 Berlin musical to help him stage a new all-serviceman show, titled (what else?) *This Is The Army.* The show-within-a-show framework

is able to accommodate a romantic subplot, involving Jerry's son Johnny (Ronald Reagan) ... and Eileen Dibble (Joan Leslie), the daughter of *Yip Yip Yaphank* alumnus Eddie Dibble (Charles Butterworth).... Guest stars include boxer Joe Louis, Kate Smith (singing "God Bless America," naturally) and Irving Berlin himself, who steals the show with his plaintive rendition of "Oh, How I Hate to Get Up in the Morning."

Calling roll among its star-studded cast, we would call special attention to Lieutenant Ronald Reagan: *This Is The Army* would be the second of his films to make its splash at the Gillioz.

With all profits going to the Army Emergency Relief Fund, the show grew into a city-wide fundraiser, preceded by an afternoon parade through the Public Square. (See figure: Parade for *This Is The Army.*) At a time when movie tickets were rarely more than forty cents per show, *This Is The Army* charged a whopping $2.20 for lower floor and first balcony seats and $1.10 for upper balcony. (See figure: Box Office for *This Is The Army.*) And citizens proudly paid.

Through the 1950s, film technology continued its advances (though some a bit gimmicky, requiring audiences to wear special 3-D stereoscopic glasses). On November 1, 1953 the theater presented *The Robe,* the first movie featuring anamorphic Cinemascope with stereophonic sound. Calling Cinemascope "The Greatest Step Forward in Entertainment History," the theater's ad made bold claims that a *News and Leader* article largely backed up:

> The much-heralded new motion picture process, 20th Century Fox's Cinemascope, makes its debut in Springfield Friday with the opening of "The Robe" at the Gillioz Theatre.
>
> The movie, which has shattered box office records and drawn a rich harvest of critical acclaim throughout the country, is the first ever made in Cinemascope.
>
> It will be shown on an enlarged, curved screen which extends from one end of the Gillioz stage to the other. No special polaroid glasses will be necessary for viewers, although the new process does give a three dimensional illusion. (See figure: *The Robe.*)

On April 22, 1953 the Gillioz showed *Bwana Devil,* the "First Feature-Length Motion Picture in Natural Vision 3Dimension," whose stereoscopic effects put "A Lion in Your Lap!" and "A Lover in your Arms!" Raising its adult prices for this "thrilling color" film, the Gillioz charged a hefty seventy-five cents. The success of *Bwana Devil*

Parade for *This Is The Army.*

spawned numerous look-alikes, such as Vincent Price's *House of Wax.* The Gillioz ad imitated the film's 3-D effects: "Right at you! The hand is at your throat…." (See figure: *House of Wax.*)

Box Office for *This Is The Army.*

Other dates and events deserve their own separate chapters. Still, we might pause to survey movies that have played on the theater's birthdays, a few of which were duly celebrated though most passed by unnoted. "This is our Anniversary Week," read an ad in the October 9, 1927 *Springfield Leader,* and "We are Celebrating Our Anniversary With the World's Greatest Production, *Ben-Hur:* Nothing Like It Before—Perhaps Never Again." Starring Ramon Navarro and May McAvoy, *Ben-Hur: A Tale of Christ* was the most ambitious (certainly the most expensive) silent film M.G.M. made, costing $3,900,000 and employing 125,000 extras. Much less ambitious, the 1936 tenth anniversary offered Loretta Young in *Ramona* and William Frawley in *Three Married Men.* Admission was thirty-six cents: fairly high for the Depression (the Electric charged twenty-six cents for its double feature while the Landers, Mozark, and Mullikin charged sixteen cents). The 1946 twentieth anniversary also passed without fanfare. Excepting the announcement, "Welcome Teachers" (presumably, the movie was "educational"), the day's ad for Rex Harrison's *Anna and the King of Siam* was undistinguished. Yet the 1956 thirtieth anniversary was regally celebrated. Promoting *The Solid Gold Cadillac,* starring Judy Holliday and Paul Douglas, the day's ad sported a theater logo newly designed for the occasion. Next to a candle-lighted birthday cake inscribed 1926-1956, a banner reads, "It's Another Gillioz

The Robe.

House of Wax.

30th Anniversary Hit!" Without hoopla, the 1966 forti-
eth anniversary featured *The Agony and the Ecstasy,* starring Charlton Heston and Rex Harrison. The 1976 fifti-
eth anniversary featured an x-rated *Alice's Erotic Adven-* *tures in Wonderland.* Through its sixtieth and seventieth
anniversaries the theater stood empty. We wait to see
what show commemorates its eightieth anniversary in
2006. (See figure: A Gathering of Gillioz Logos.)

A Gathering of Gillioz Logos.

6. Ronald Reagan at the Gillioz

On June 6, 1952 Ronald Reagan and his new wife, Nancy Davis, arrived in Springfield, Missouri in the personal rail car of L. B. Clary—owner of the Frisco line—to attend the world premiere of *The Winning Team,* a film celebrating the St. Louis Cardinal's legendary pitcher, Grover Cleveland Alexander. (See figure: Stars Arrive in Springfield.) In a curious twist of fate, Alexander and his 1926 Cardinals had been featured on the Gillioz Theatre's own opening night: flown in from New York, one of the evening's newsreels featured him beating the Yankees in game six of the World Series. For the second time, then, and on the two most momentous days in the theater's history, the pitcher's story graced its silver screen.

The movie starred Ronald Reagan as the hard-throwing, hard-drinking Alexander. Reagan's co-star, the popular Doris Day, portrayed Grover's loyal wife Aimee, who stuck by her man through his struggles with alcohol (hence the title, *Winning Team*). (See figure: *The Winning Team.*) In his *All Movie Guide,* Hal Erickson offers a synopsis:

> While the basic milestones of Alexander's career are adhered to, the film is a typical Hollywood blend of fact and fancy.... While playing in the minors, Alexander is hit on the head by a batted ball, resulting in the dizziness and double vision that would ever after plague him. After toting up a record of 28 wins with the Philadelphia Phillies, Alex is traded to the Cubs, but World War 1 intervenes. On the battlefield, Alex suffers a recurrence of his double vision; and when he plays his first postwar game with the Cubs, he collapses on the field.... When the dizzy spells continue, Alex turns to drink. Branded an "alky," he descends to the depths of a House of David-style team, thence to the humiliation of carnival side shows. With the help and support of both Aimee and his old pal Rogers Hornsby, Alex stages a spectacular comeback, striking out Yankee Tony Lazzeri during the 1926 World Series and leading his team to victory.

Stars Arrive in Springfield.

Both Reagan and Day were "true ball fans," a fact that helped bail out what some have called a lackluster script: "Reagan is a skillful amateur player who makes himself plausible as a big league pitcher," reported the June 1 *News and Leader:* "By coincidence it was on the sandlots of Galesburg, a hometown of his youth where Alex the Great first pitched professional ball, that Ronnie first learned the game." And "Doris is a gal who will drop anything, even a shopping tour for a baseball game. She can rattle off players' batting averages and other statistics like a true sports fan," noted the *News and Leader.*

For the movie's premiere, Warner Bros. had settled upon a time and place that would get the movie maximum exposure: the weekend of June 6 in Springfield, Missouri. For Springfield was slated to host another important event that weekend, one whose own political star would draw huge crowds, guaranteeing national press coverage. President Harry S Truman was to spend that weekend in town celebrating the reunion of the 35th Division of the Missouri and Kansas National Guard. A WWI Captain of artillery in that division, President Truman would attend with his cousin, retired Army Major General Ralph Truman; himself a former 35th Division commander, Ralph Truman had retired to Springfield, where he had lived in the 1920s (his son

The Winning Team.

son, "film actor and widely known dancer" and his wife, Miriam Franklin; "the lovely musical comedy star," Virginia Gibson; and Mrs. Grover Cleveland Alexander, who "had acted as a technical advisor while the movie was being made" (Walker 23). (See figure: "Society Star Visitors.")

Though not mentioned above, the driving force behind the 35th Division's Springfield reunion (and, by extension, behind the movie's Springfield premiere) was the city's Shrine lodge and its well-connected membership: the President's cousin, General Ralph Truman, was a Mason, as was the President. Ralph McCoy, Ralph Foster, and Lester E. Cox were also Masons, and it was they who secured the Shrine Mosque for reunion events, including the Friday evening Presidential Ball and Truman's Saturday afternoon address. (See figure: Foster and Truman at the Shrine Mosque.) As Walker writes, "Luckily, I found that the major domo in charge of everything was a very wealthy industrialist named Lester Cox who, I discovered, had only to pick up a telephone receiver to solve any of my problems" (22). When Mr. Cox called, people sprang to attention.

But enough of potentates. Our story unfolds through the recollections of a few local boys, starting with Ronald and Nancy's young chauffeur, Edwin Rice.

ॐ ॐ

Of course there was going to be a parade, and George Thompson (owner of Thompson's Cadillac, whose business sat just east of the Mosque) was providing cars for all the dignitaries. As parade organizer, Thompson asked his young neighbor, Edwin "Cookie" Rice, if he would like to "drive a couple of movie stars around for a few days beginning on June 5." Cookie didn't bother to ask who the stars were going to be. A Drury College sophomore, Cookie was interested in what just about every other young man he knew was interested in: girls and cars. He didn't care so much about meeting movie stars, what made him happy was getting to drive a brand-spanking new Cadillac convertible.

Cookie picked up the Reagans at the Frisco rail station on Thursday evening and took them to the Warner Bros. headquarters, which was set up at the Kentwood Arms Hotel. His first and lasting impression of the recently-wedded couple was how gracious they were and how much in love they seemed to be. At the time, Nancy was very pregnant with Patty and Ron "absolutely doted on her." The Reagans asked Cookie to pick them up later and take them to what the *Daily News* described as a "double-barreled street dance held in the Public Square and on Commercial Street." Cookie picked them up and deposited them at the square at 10:25 p.m. to enjoy the dancing. (See insert: "Street Dance" Protested.) Afterwards he drove them back to the Kentwood Arms. The following day would be busy, and the couple asked Cookie to

attended Southwest Teachers College for two years until his appointment to West Point). Warner Bros. publicist Don Walker, who personally coordinated the movie's premiere events, offered Hollywood's take on the affair, writing, "It was not exactly a coincidence that Warner Bros. decided to stage the world premiere" in Springfield, nor was it a "coincidence that the premiere was to take place the same time as the annual reunion of the 35th Division" (22):

> The fact that a former Warner Bros. sales executive, Ralph McCoy who then lived in Springfield, also happened to be chairman of the entertainment committee for the reunion, may have had something to do with the decision. And Warner officials did not overlook the fact that the big Fox Midwest circuit, with headquarters in Kansas City, was adding its pressure since it owned all the principal theatres in Springfield. (Walker 22)

Yet "the clincher came when the President announced that he would attend the reunion in person" (Walker 22), as this would bring a passel of media and a crowd of dignitaries including Forrest Smith, Governor of Missouri, Sid McMath, Governor of Arkansas, General Harry Vaughan, the President's military advisor, and members of the Truman family (Walker 23). For its part Warner Bros. sent a Hollywood contingent headed by Ronald Reagan and his wife, actress Nancy Davis; Gene Nel-

"Society Star Visitors."

Cookie drove the couple to the Gillioz for the first show and then back to the hotel to get refreshed for the 7:00 p.m. second showing. Cookie then took them back to the Gillioz, parked the Caddy two blocks away, and waited.

Crowds gathered that evening to see the movie stars arrive, pose, and be interviewed. That same evening, Harold and Ruth May grabbed their theater tickets, got their son, Gary, and drove downtown. Just eight years old, Gary was excited at the prospect of seeing the movie, but even more excited to see his hero in the flesh. After all, Gary had grown up watching Ronald Reagan the cavalry officer and Ronald Reagan the gridiron hero. He clutched his ticket, #248, in a tight fist during the short wait to enter the Gillioz. After Gary and his parents took their seats on the east side of the orchestra floor, Gary waited anxiously for his hero to appear. He remembers cheering with the rest of the crowd as Ronald Reagan and Nancy Davis took the stage. He doesn't remember much about what the future president said; he recalls that Reagan spoke a few words and introduced Mrs. Grover Cleveland Alexander. They were then joined on stage by the Warner Bros. dancers, Virginia Gibson and Gene Nelson. Gibson and Nelson put on a short stage show, during which Ronald and Nancy sat in the forward box seat on the east wing of the balcony. Gary remembers this, because he kept looking up to see his hero. He recalls feeling awestruck, being so close to his idol. Gary May took his premiere ticket home and has kept it in perfect condition since.

After the premiere Cookie drove Ronald and Nancy over to the Abou Ben Adhem Shrine Mosque for the Presidential Ball and then back to the Kentwood Arms at 10:30 p.m. for a second reception. Throughout their long day the couple never lost their manners or kind smiles. They thanked Cookie and asked if he were to drive them in the parade the following day. He told them he was and would see them in the morning. Later that evening at the Kentwood, Lester E. Cox presented Reagan with an

pick them up early for a press conference promoting the movie.

After the next morning's press conference, Cookie dropped Mr. Reagan off at a meeting with local businessmen and drove Nancy over to Heers for some shopping. Later in the day he and Nancy picked up Ron and drove back to the hotel. That afternoon at 4:00 p.m. *The Winning Team* would premiere "at both the Fox and Gillioz theaters for President Truman and his buddies of the 35th Division—with admittance by special invitation only," as the *News and Leader* reported. Though the Gillioz was the theater first chosen (being the more glamorous of the two), the "advance ticket sales ... were so brisk" that a second theater was added "and a third theater could have been sold out had the schedule been possible" (Walker 23). Yet there were no jealousies between the Gillioz and the Fox-Electric, as they were both operated by Fox Midwest. While the Gillioz officially hosted the Reagans and Mrs. Alexander, the Fox-Electric had its own concurrent showings at four, seven, and nine that evening. (The Gillioz alone would show *The Winning Team* for the remainder of the week; on June 20, the movie was released nationwide.)

"Street Dance" Protested. In the June 6, 1952 *Daily News* the pastors of two local churches took out an advertisement expressing opposition to the "public dance" scheduled that evening:

> Temple Baptist and Hamlin Memorial Baptist Churches openly and publicly express their opposition to the roping off of certain sections of Springfield for the purpose of a public dance.
>
> We regret that the newly elected City Council has not only tabled the Resolution of Protest by the Greene County Baptist Association, but has also broken the consistent precedent of former councils which refused to rope off any street for any purpose.

The pastors had a point. Precedent was on their side and there was no reason for the community to break its own rules, not even for a President of the United States.

HONORED BY SHRINE— During the 35th Division reunion here President Truman (center) was presented a red and gold fez, along with an Abou Ben Adhem life membership, which he is holding, as he is flanked by the Shriners who presented them. At the right is Potentate Ralph Foster and at left is James H. (Jim) Saunders, recorder.

—News and Leader Staff Photo

Foster and Truman at the Shrine Mosque.

"Ozark Hillbilly Award." "HillBilly Ronald," read a headline in the June 7 *Leader and Press:*

> In his acceptance, Reagan noted that it is good for Hollywood personalities to get away from their place of work once in awhile and meet people. "We're all from places like Illinois and Indiana and Missouri," he said, "and we're trying to be good citizens." He said he would treasure the hillbilly award as a souvenir of his trip here.

The next morning over breakfast, Reagan would have read the review by local *Daily News* movie critic, Dale Freeman:

> With huge kleig lights blazing out a Hollywood-style entrance for four motion picture stars, thousands of movie fans last night turned out for a double-barreled world premiere of "The Winning team." ...
>
> It was the first glimpse of any movie stars for many motion picture followers and they virtually blocked the street in front of the Gillioz as Hollywood visitors arrived—in big-time premiere manner—in convertibles at 8:00 p.m....
>
> As for "The Winning Team," it is an exceptionally good sports movie and should prove to be one of the most popular baseball pictures of all times.
>
> It especially will appeal to sports fans, who will get a chance to see more actual baseball ... than in similar pictures about the lives of athletic greats.
>
> It's strictly a two-star picture, with Reagan and the pert Doris Day ... carrying the brunt of the acting....
>
> There seems to be a bit too much sob stuff for sports fans but average movie goers—if there is such a thing—probably will go for the picture in its entirety.
>
> But "The Winning Team" pulls no punches.

It shows Alexander when he's up and Alexander when he is at the bottom. It tells how old John Barleycorn got the best of him.... Mrs. Alexander, herself, feels that Reagan did a great job in portraying her husband.

And his acting still is the homey, I'm-like-the-neighbor-next-door type which has sold him to movies fans for lo these many years.

Not bad. The evening paper offered a similar selection of qualified praise: "'The Winning Team' appeared well-received," noted the June 7 *Leader and Press:* "the movie has plenty of color, a fair love story, some above-average drama and—above all—realism." The article ends, "As far as sports pictures go, 'The Winning Team' probably is one of the best to come out of Hollywood in a long time." Again, not bad. But there wouldn't have been much time for musing over movie reviews, as the day remained jam-packed with activity.

Saturday June 7, 1952 dawned bright, clear, and very hot in Springfield. Then seventeen years old, Harold Bengsch—future Greene County Commissioner—and his softball team had a game that morning in Doling Park. Before the game his coach called the team together for a pep talk. "Boys," Bengsch remembers him saying, "the President of the United States and Ronald Reagan will be in the parade today here in town. If we can whip these guys quick, we can get down to the Square in time to see them." The boys did whip them soundly, and quickly. Bengsch and about twelve of his teammates made it to the Square just in time. He can't say if it was because of their baseball uniforms or their skill at maneuvering through the crowds, but they managed to see the parade from the front row. Some 250,000 others watched, too, as President Truman walked the entire three-mile route to shouts of "Give 'em Hell, Harry!" (Walker 24). (See figure: Truman Marching.) According to the June 8 *News and Leader,* this "was the largest crowd in the history of Springfield." Indeed, the newspaper predicted that "the parade and reunion ... will be long remembered as the biggest event in the city's history." (See insert: "Welcome Mr. President!")

Cookie picked up the Reagans that morning, as scheduled. He recalls a pregnant Nancy climbing into the back seat and sitting up on the rear deck. (See figure: The Reagans on Parade.) There she was able to lean back, which provided her some relief from Patty who was bearing down on her. Cookie remembers her saying, "This is the best I've felt in weeks." The parade was long and oppressively hot, yet the couple never lost their charm. They asked Cookie about himself during the long, slow drive, showing interest in his studies and in his life in general. After the parade, Cookie took them back to the Kentwood Arms, thanked them, and said goodbye. Cookie wouldn't see them again. Yet Edwin Rice's memories remain fond: "Reagan really wanted the premiere to go well and did all he could to make sure of it. He had a way

Welcome, Mr. President! *Throwing in some advice to Springfieldians (who were expected to be on their best behavior), the June 6 **Leader and Press** offered the following letter of welcome:*

Welcome, Mr. President!

Springfield is honored to have the chief executive as a visitor.

Welcome also, Governor Smith, Governor McMath,... generals and officers of lesser rank here either as honored guests or in the performance of duties connected with the 35th Division Reunion.

Welcome, Mr. and Mrs. Ronald Reagan.... Your presence adds a great deal of luster to the premiere of "The Winning Team," which in turn adds prestige to the 35th Division Reunion.

Welcome, 35th Division veterans ... and visitors wherever you come from and whatever your purpose in coming to our city.

Whew! Does that include everyone?

We hope so, and we hope it serves to illustrate the size and the scope of the 35th Division Reunion. It would be a big event for a city a half-dozen times as large as Springfield, and it represents a terrific undertaking for a community of 75,000.

... They have honored us by accepting our invitation to attend the reunion, and in turn they have placed a big responsibility on the shoulders of all of us.

The eyes of the nation, and of much of the world, will be on Springfield for the next three days.... With the President and his staff as our guests, ... Springfield is very much in the limelight.

Not only will visiting newspapermen and radio reporters send out their impressions of Springfield ... but visitors by the thousands will get an impression, good or bad, firsthand during the reunion.

Our patience may be tried many times in the next few days, simple because it will be a hectic, activity-packed period when most of us will wish we had a half-dozen hands and the talents of a genius to do the things that must be done.

The impression we make on our visitors is up to us, collectively and individually.

*Anticipating the crowds, the **Leader and Press** also gave what advice it could for watching the next day's parade:*

Where will be the best place to see the big parade tomorrow? Will I have to park my car along the route sometime to-night to have a ringside seat? What are the odds of seeing the President even if I do get to the parade area? These are the questions uppermost in the minds of some 250,000 Ozarkians who will flood Springfield tomorrow morning for the 10 o'clock parade. And there's nobody, repeat NOBODY, who knows the answers....

This much at least the newspaper could tell: "An alert bomb will be set off at 9:55 to put everyone at "ready." A second bomb explosion will announce the official start...."

of simplifying a conversation with a gentle nature. He smiled from the inside out."

That Friday evening in 1952, when the film star shook hands with the nation's President on the stage of the Springfield Shrine Mosque, a series of coincidences were set in motion whose full realization would come some thirty-five years later, almost to the day. Truman, America's first Cold War President, was here joined by Reagan, who would become America's last Cold War President, having the honor of presiding over the collapse of the Soviet Bloc.

We need to remind ourselves of the historical setting. The nation was in the midst of its Cold War with the Soviet Union. The nation was also in the midst of the Korean War. And Truman's Democratic Party was in the midst of an election campaign, one that they would lose

some months later in a landslide to General Dwight D. Eisenhower. (Reagan would of course jump at the chance to stump with the President, as the Hollywood star— then a Democrat and, as always, politically engaged— had campaigned for Truman in 1948.) More than for a reunion with army buddies, Truman came to the Shrine Mosque to deliver a major, nationally-broadcast political speech, "one of the most serious analyses of international affairs" that he had ever made, according to the June 8 *News and Leader*. In his address, Truman sought to affirm his administration's foreign policy, defend his military strategy in Korea, and justify the tax burdens that these policies had placed upon the American people. A copy is preserved in the History Museum for Springfield-Greene County; it is worth some comment.

In his radio address, the President gave a brief his-

Truman Marching.

tory of his foreign policy of "active containment" —the so-called Truman Doctrine—and the "great military effort in time of peace" that it entailed. Meeting the Soviet challenge "meant doubling or tripling the budget, increasing taxes heavily, and imposing various kinds of economic controls. It meant a great change in our normal peacetime way of doing things." Indeed, the communist invasion of "the Republic of Korea ... demonstrated to all free nations that they had to have much stronger defenses to prevent Soviet conquest." His speech continued:

> As a result, the free nations have been moving... to build bigger defenses. Our own country has taken the lead, because we are the strongest of the free nations. We have made a lot of progress... . We still have a long way to go in many respects, but if we stick to our course we can create the kind of strong, free world that we need to guarantee security and peace.
>
> We can win the peace. And we are going to win the peace.

Truman's memorable phrase, "We can win the peace," became his legacy to all later presidents who would find themselves contemplating, enmeshed in, or seeking to extricate themselves and our nation's military from foreign conflicts. Yet it was Reagan who would say it most and, in the end, who actually did "win the peace" —that is, win the Cold War that Truman himself had first declared.

Standing before Berlin's historic Brandenburg Gate on June 12, 1987, President Reagan addressed his Soviet counterpart in his own most memorable speech: "General Secretary Gorbachev, if you seek peace, if you seek prosperity for the Soviet Union and Eastern Europe ... come here to this gate! Mr. Gorbachev, open this gate! Mr. Gorbachev, tear down this wall!" In so doing, Reagan was overseeing the completion of what Truman had begun.

Returning to 1952, the nation was indeed in both a "hot" and a "cold" war. In contrast with local festivities, the week's newspaper headlines painted a consistently gloomy world picture: "Red Jets Buzz American Plane," "Koje Prisoners Show Defiance," "GI Fugitive Flees Reds," "Commies Claim Allies Trying to Halt Talks," "Allied Units Forced Back by Red Fire," and so on. One poignant article reports that "thousands of fearful Germans struggled to flee from Soviet-held East Germany last night.... A stream of human misery poured west from the Soviet zone, slipping past Russian sentries and people's police at the risk of death in the Red's new frontier security belt...." And yet one further headline in the June 1 *News and Leader* catches our attention, "Reds Bit

Off on Ball Film." As it pertains to *The Winning Team,* we have a civic duty to report it:

> Baffled by news from Hollywood that a motion picture was being made featuring "murderer's row," Moscow is distorting the reports into anti-American propaganda.
>
> Shortwave radio owners and listeners in Southern California report the Red radio propagandists are charging that "The Winning Team," which has a murderer's row as well as Warner Bros. stars Doris Day, Ronald Reagan and Frank Lovejoy, is being made for the deliberate glorification of "Yankee murderers, bandits—all in the pay of Wall Street." ... The Russian commentator, who obviously knew nothing about baseball, said in English:
>
> "Wall Street, which uses a private police army known as the FBI as well as gunmen and gangsters to maintain terroristic control over enslaved and exploited American workers, is brazenly glorifying the country's most notorious murderers. Their crimes will be the subject of a movie which will be used to create fear in the minds of all who would shake off the capitalist yoke.
>
> "These murderers are members of a notorious underworld gang known as the New York Yankees."

Surely even the most die-hard Cardinals fan wouldn't go that far. Tongue-in-cheek, the article assures readers that all the film's acting and ball-playing stars "are solid American citizens" and that "none of the players feels that he is being exploited by Wall Street." True, and yet there's something fitting about Reagan and baseball being attacked in the same breath by 1950s Soviet radio propagandists. What, after all, is more American than baseball? And who more Red, White, and Blue than Ronald?

When we began our research, we had assumed that three movies held their world premieres at the Gillioz: *Jesse James, The Shepherd of the Hills,* and *The Winning Team.* Though the first two premiered elsewhere, yet we found a replacement for one. As we have noted, the theater's first world premiere was *Swing Your Lady,* a film listing Reagan among its stars. We found that *The Winning Team* was a co-premiere, shared by the Gillioz and Fox-Electric. And we are pleased to have found a third premiere, previously unmentioned. Of all the little facts and forgotten tidbits that our history has uncovered, this last may be the most valuable as it corrects the nation's authoritative source regarding premiere dates and locations. Evidently the movie's first run was not in New York City on July 9, 1952, as listed by the American Film Institute; rather, it showed at the Gillioz on July 4, where it ran through July 11.

We speak of Warner Brothers' Technicolor "campus" musical, *She's Working Her Way Through College,* starring Virginia Mayo, Gene Nelson, and Ronald Reagan. (Who would have guessed that he'd star in all three of the theater's world premieres?) Here's Hal Erickson on the plot:

> *She's Working Her Way through College* is a completely de-politicized remake of the liberal-minded comedy, *The Male Animal.* Virginia Mayo

The Reagans on Parade.

She's Working Her Way Through College.

Mayo's character, Angela Gardner (a. k. a. Hot Garters Gertie) helps the school's struggling drama department stage a jazzy musical replete with some hot dance numbers. Though scandalized at the prospect, the local trustees take a lesson from Reagan's character, Professor Palmer, regarding academic and artistic freedom. Yet lying in the implicit background of such an apparently innocent musical romp was Joseph McCarthy's House Un-American Activities Committee, which was operating in high-gear in 1952, pressuring Hollywood to toe a strict party line. In *The Male Animal* (1942), "the trustees of Midwestern University … forced three teachers out of their jobs for being suspected communists" (Gilbert). Though the 1952 Hollywood remake displaced the crisis from politics to sexual morality, *She's Working Her Way Through College* remains an allegory on the times. Whereas Reagan despised communism, he loved freedom far more and defended its expression through the arts. In its implicit message, then, the film doesn't seem quite as apolitical as Erickson avers. And, appropriately enough, it first showed in Springfield on firecracker Fourth of July, 1952.

This would be less than a month after *The Winning Team* had premiered, while the city was still congratulating itself over the affair. In its June 29 newspaper ad the theater announced "News Reel Shots of the Visiting Stars at the World Premiere in Springfield." Sporting a redesigned theater logo, a second ad immediately follows:

THE GILLIOZ WORLD PREMIERE THEATRE
Awarded Another
World Premiere
for your Holiday Entertainment
Warner Bros. Big Summertime Musical!

"She's Working Her Way Through College"

Starring those two wonderful stars who appeared in person during the 35th Division Reunion and who endeared themselves to all Springfieldians—co-starring with them is that luscious beauty Virginia Mayo.

This same redesigned logo reappeared on a larger ad for July 4. (See figure: *She's Working Her Way Through College.*)

So, why did *She's Working Her Way Through College* first show in Springfield? We assume that Warner Bros. and its stars, Reagan and Nelson, were anxious to show their gratitude to Springfield and the Gillioz for such lavish hospitality. The movie's "big" premiere could go on in New York; in the meantime, the Gillioz would have its own showing, unheralded in the nation's newspapers. It would be the city's little secret, a kindness on the part of Warner Bros.

plays an exotic dancer who decides to improve her mind; she enrolls in a college where professor Ronald Reagan teaches English. In between Virginia's lively musical numbers, the film concentrates on an old rivalry between the bookish Reagan and onetime college football jock Don DeFore (who'd played a bit role in *The Male Animal*). When the college trustees oppose Ms. Mayo's presence on campus, Reagan staunchly defends her right to an education. In the original *Male Animal,* the climactic scene involved a controversial public reading of a letter by anarchist Bartolomeo Vanzetti; in She's Working Her Way Through College, Reagan stands up at a public assembly to convince the populace that exotic dancers have the same rights as anyone else. Of course, Ronald Reagan could take a political stance if he wanted to … but not in this film.

So, to Ronald Reagan the cavalry officer and Ronald Reagan the gridiron hero we must add Ronald Reagan the English professor, who teaches at Midwest State.

7. The Closing

Jim Wunderle remembers growing up in the mid-1960s and working at the Gillioz:

> When I was in junior high, 1965-1967, the happening place to be on Saturday afternoon was downtown.... The Square was teeming on Saturdays back then and it was the social event of the week for junior high kids.... We'd catch a bus or get a parent to drive us downtown, hook up with some of our other pals and hit the square. A stop at the A&W Root Beer stand was inevitable.... After snacks, we would head to the movies. The Gillioz was the place to be. And it was always packed....
>
> In '76 I got a job at the Gillioz. I was the "last janitor" there and worked there until the day she closed.... By the time I started working there in 1976, things were rather bleak. Downtown had all dried up.... We had our share of big pictures, though. Dino DeLaurentes' remake of "King Kong" opened in November of 1976 and it was huge. As much as I loved the Gillioz, you've got understand it's in a janitor's best interest to have a smaller audience. So I wasn't all that thrilled with the crowd-pleasing super hits.
>
> The summer of 1977 was pure hell for me. We ran "Smokey and the Bandit" nearly all summer and it sold out on a regular basis. It got so busy they had to open the bane of my existence, the balcony. It was much harder to clean than the main auditorium and was only opened when the crowd was huge. To this day I hate that film....
> By the late 1970s, in addition to playing mainstream films, the Gillioz played some bizarre features as well. "Andy Warhol's Frankenstein" ran in 3-D.... Roman Pulanski's "The Tenant" ... ran for a week. And then there was the porno. It was soft-core but porno nonetheless. I remember ... the adult version of "Pinocchio" and "Alice in Wonderland"....
>
> As the downward spiral of the Gillioz continued, we all knew it was a matter of time.... Mann

Theaters bought it, and then it went to Kansas City based Dickinson Theaters. Nobody wanted to spend money to fix it up. The seats were in disrepair and the paint was peeling. The place was huge and most of the time filled less than five percent of its capacity. She was all but dead.

On July 22, 1980, as Wunderle cleaned up from the last performance of *La Traviata,* his co-worker Therese Collins came to him crying, for "when the opera was over, the Gillioz was too." Added Wunderle, "Many of us cried."

For three sultry evenings in July, the Springfield Regional Opera had transported the old Gillioz Theatre Beautiful—by then a tattered, leaking, empty movie house, having shown its last film, *The Amityville Horror,* on July 15—back to its glory days as a live stage. Prior to the performance of Verdi, the Opera's volunteers faced the herculean task of cleaning a stage and pit that hadn't been used in over a decade. Dust, dirt, and broken equipment had piled behind the fixed screen. Yet the stage cleaned up well enough. In an appreciative review run in the July 20, 1980 *News-Leader* Bil Tatum declared the production "a triumph," a "show to be proud of," indeed "a class act for Springfield" (8B). Tatum's only complaint concerned Act III, "damaged most by a two-dancer tarantella that calls for a band of gypsies whirling in abandon (the stage simply wouldn't accommodate them)." The Springfield Regional Opera should have been warned: the Gillioz stage was never built for large-scale operatic performances. (Ironically, the theater's swan-song was likely the largest serious production it had ever staged.)

The theater's demise was fated. It's not just that the Gillioz had decayed, but that the Public Square and the streets around it fell on hard times, as well. To grasp this decay and its causes, we need to cast our glance backward. Taking September 7, 1957 as not too arbitrary a date, we might imagine ourselves standing on the corner of Sunshine Street and Glenstone Avenue. On this day, Springfield celebrated its selection as an "All America City," one of eleven so honored by *Look* magazine.

(See insert: Springfield, "All America City.") Here, on the corner of Sunshine and Glenstone, we would be standing at the city's new geographic and population center. You see, our "All America City" had recently completed its largest land annexation to date, making Battlefield Road its new southern border. Springfieldians living at the time could recall when areas south of Grand Street were still farmed; most remembered when Sunshine marked the city's southern edge. The city was expanding like a super nova. Why so?

In Springfield as across America the nation's GIs had returned home en masse, moving into new, affordable homes funded by the loan program of the Veterans' Administration (Ebner 379); many of these were built on the outskirts of towns (in Springfield, much of this construction was south of Sunshine), where land was plentiful and cheap. By 1957 the nation's suburbs had grown from 35 million to a hefty 84 million people (Baldassare 477). And as soon as the GIs returned home they wanted their automobiles: like suburban housing these, too, had become

Springfield, "All America City." In the January 22, 1957 issue of *Look* magazine, Springfield was named one of eleven "All America Cities" chosen for "energetic, purposeful, and intelligent citizen effort" in tackling "significant problems" (32). (On September 7, the city celebrated its nomination with a parade and other festivities.) Springfieldians earned the award for having "voted in a council-manager government" (35) and for supporting other pieces of expensive legislation:

> They backed a progressive program that include a $7¾ million school-construction bond issue, a $10 million sewer-reconstruction program, a $10 million urban trafficway project, an $11 million city power plant. They added fire stations, reorganized city departments and peacefully integrated Negroes in the public schools and in Southwest Missouri State College. (35)

It is interesting to note what those "significant problems" were that Springfield and the other ten cities had faced: "the winners reveal three major problems common to cities all over the country. They are: rapid community growth and suburban expansion, lethargy and decay resulting in the blight of old cities, and the necessity to improve the machinery of government" (32).

more affordable. People wanted to "drive fast and travel far" ("Oil").

Of course, there was still the Public Square downtown (from where we were standing, perhaps we should say "uptown") where it was still fashionable to eat and shop. But, you know, there just wasn't enough *parking*. In 1957 "Springfield had become sophisticated enough to hire

Springfield Drive-In.

KYTV Van.

meter maids" (DD138). True, but the meter maids were busy patrolling downtown and we were standing on the corner of Sunshine and Glenstone, just north of the new Plaza Shopping Center. Down here, there was more than enough parking—and stores. There was also the Tower Theatre, one of the latest rivals to the downtown Gillioz. Opened in 1947 as the Park-In Theatre, its very name announced the new theater's come-on: one could actually *park in front of it*. And in the fields just to the northeast (where the Corporate Center stands in 2006) was the Springfield Drive-In: from where we were standing, you could see the big concrete movie screen. (See figure: Springfield Drive-In.) There, you could watch a movie *and never leave your car*. Other drive-ins would arrive: the Hi M Drive-In on West Republic Road, the Holiday Drive-In on East Kearney, the Queen City Twin Drive-In on East Sunshine, and the Sunset Drive-In on West Chestnut.

While we are still in the Fifties, we might pause to mention that other monstrous rival to the Gillioz (as it has proved to the movie industry generally): television. By 1957 "Americans were purchasing twenty thousand TVs a day" (Baughman 30); already, two-thirds of American families owned one. In our own "All America City," Springfield, "homes with television increased from 3% in 1953 to 95% in 1959" (R120). (See figure: KYTV Van.) Though families still made the effort to go downtown for weekend shopping and a movie, "a young husband told the *Saturday Evening Post* early in 1952 that going to the movies … had become a logistical nightmare" (Baughman 36). Part of this "logistical nightmare," doubtless,

was parking. Yet America's "automobile generation" was already busy siring its succeeding generation of couch potatoes, as "average weekly motion picture attendance fell from 90 million in 1948 to 47 million in 1956" (Baughman 74).

In the meantime Springfield was growing. Just how fast? From 66,700 in 1950 the city's population grew to 133,000 in 1970. This more-than-doubling had many causes, though land annexation was foremost. After 1955, when the city experienced its largest expansion, the process of annexation continued in 1964, 1966, 1967, 1968, 1969, 1972, 1976, and 1980. Again, land on the city's outskirts was cheap and new buildings could be built-to-suit (much cheaper than renovating older inner-city structures). People enjoyed the suburb's quasi-rural feel and the car got them in and out of town at will (indeed, the multi-car family could scatter in multiple directions at once). Yet the outlying developments wanted big-city services like police, fire, recreation, and sanitation. Annexation provided such services to the new developments while increasing the city's tax base: win-win, as they say. So, like the living rings of a tree, the city grew outward while the town center rotted.

Let's move forward now a little in time, imagining that we stood a mile or so farther south on the corner of Battlefield and Glenstone. To give ourselves something to celebrate, let's make the date July 4, 1976, our nation's bicentennial. Looking to the northwest we would behold not the last but certainly the largest nail in the Gillioz Theatre's coffin: Battlefield Mall. As Ozarks historian

Park Central Square.

2000" (R257). Fifty years prior the Gillioz Theatre opened near the Public Square, following the well-tried formula for successful business: after shopping, people stopped to see a movie. In the new Battlefield Mall the Century 21 Theatre followed this same economic formula.

In 1926, America was completing its demographic shift from a primarily rural to an urban culture; by 1976 America was completing its further shift from a primarily urban to a suburban culture, as "roughly half" of America's metropolitan population now "lived in the suburban ring" (Guest 402). By 1976 Springfield had annexed most of its suburbs.

Milton D. Rafferty notes, "Rapid growth on South Glenstone began in 1972 when Simon and Associates (now the Simon Property Group) completed the Battlefield Mall, the Ozarks' largest regional shopping center. The mall helped tilt Springfield's commercial activity and traffic pattern to the southeast. In 1974 there were sixty-one businesses operating in the Battlefield Mall ... in 1982, one hundred and fifty businesses operated in the mall, a level that had increased to one hundred and seventy by Nixa, Ozark, and other outlying towns were experiencing their own explosions in population and development. Though their old-timers might rankle at the thought, their fair hamlets had become bedroom communities for Springfield's commuters. Greene and Christian counties were turning into an affluent, progressive metropolitan area—the fastest growing in Missouri.

And while we are still in the Seventies, we might pause to mention a further development within the

The Gillioz in Ruin.

movie industry, one that would soon doom the Century 21 (and the Tower Theatre), as well. Like the Gillioz, the Century 21 Theatre was built as a large one-screen theater. By the 1970s such single-screen houses were already threatened by the new multi-screen theaters, which offered "more versatility to theater owners" and "a virtual smorgasbord to the patron" (Barnes). The Petite 3 Theatre opened in 1973; it would be followed by the Battlefield Mall 6 Cinemas, the Campbell 16 Cine on South Avenue, the Fremont 3 Theatre on Battlefield Road, the North Town 4 Theatre on Kearney, and the Springfield 8 Cinemas on East Montclair.

Moving back north, let's now imagine ourselves standing on the northeast corner of Park Central Square. Intersected by South Avenue and St. Louis Street, Park Central Square stands where the Public Square *used* to be, where Historic Route 66 *used* to run. (See figure: Park Central Square.) True, the automobile at one time brought audiences to downtown theaters like the Gillioz. Yet the automobile proved too successful, too numerous for such urban centers to accommodate, and downtown businesses learned that the streets leading into the city center now led a bit more smoothly out. Desperate to revitalize the downtown merchant district, its businesses pulled together and, using private money, turned the old Square into a pedestrian mall, closing it to car traffic. If downtown Springfield (specifically the Woodruff Building on St. Louis) could legitimately claim to be "the birthplace of Route 66," it could now also claim to be the road's official executioner.

In hindsight, Park Central Square was a bad idea. The historic downtown could not compete with the suburban malls by offering a poor imitation of the same; eventually, the city center would revitalize itself by emphasizing its historic, cultural, and aesthetic difference, by stripping off the aluminum façades hiding the once-noble brick and terra-cotta store fronts—in sum, by offering a lively alternative to the franchise-dominated suburban mall culture. At the time, though, Springfield's downtown businesses didn't know this. When the Square reopened to traffic in 1988 (financed this time by tax dollars), the damage had been done. Most of the old businesses had locked up and walked off.

And the Gillioz was showing signs of neglect even in the Sixties, when the carpeting had become worn and stained, the draperies torn and faded and equipment broken down; where there had been a drinking fountain there was now an empty wall space with plumbing pipes exposed. At the time, most patrons didn't seem to notice or much mind. After 1976, though, the Gillioz was running lonely ads for mostly "B" films and re-runs while the city's newer multi-screen theaters showed the latest releases.

The Gillioz in Ruin.

In 1980, Dickinson Theatres bought the Gillioz and several other houses from Mann Theatres Corporation, their owner since 1973. The Mann Theatres' business log for January 31, 1980—the last day that its movies showed in Springfield—paints a wintry picture. The Petite 3 was showing *Apocalypse Now, The Jerk,* and *The Muppet Movie.* The North Town was showing *The Rose, Kramer Vs. Kramer,* and *The Prizefighter.* And the Gillioz showed *Wilderness Family II.* On that day the Gillioz made barely $100 in tickets and concessions. (The weather didn't help, as it was an icy thirteen degrees outside and snowing; still, it was snowing at the other Mann theaters and they hadn't performed so poorly.) When Dickinson Theatres bought the Gillioz in a package deal, the corporation was aware of the theater's shabby finances and furnishings, aware that it couldn't turn a profit. Almost from the beginning, Dickinson looked to sell off or donate whatever remained of value; it's a marvel that the Gillioz remained open for another half year.

As we end this chapter, let's call the date October 11, 1986, the Gillioz Theatre's sixtieth birthday. Though abandoned (like some other buildings downtown), the Gillioz wasn't entirely vacant, as the city's homeless had

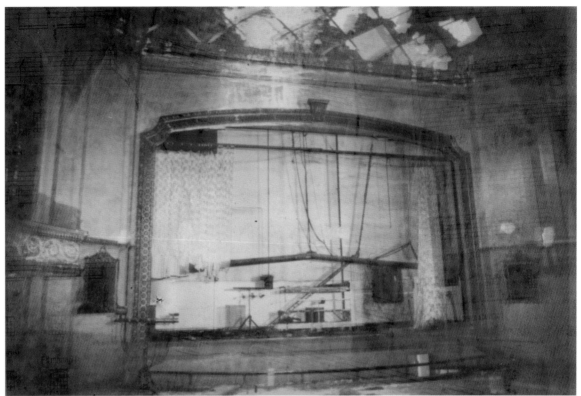

The Gillioz in Ruin.

moved in, bringing their own sad furnishings: oil barrels for burning fires, soiled pillows and bedding. Used needles and empty Everclear bottles lay scattered about. (See figures: The Gillioz in Ruin.) Yet the vagrants proved honorable in their way, informing against vandals who came to steal the building's remaining fixtures. And some in the community still cared. Sam Freeman, a lawyer and downtown businessman who personally looked after the Gillioz and nearby buildings, came to rely on the theater's vagrant watchmen. Nancy Brown Dornan, Gary Ellison, and Jim D. Morris would walk past the shabby heap, wondering what miracle it would take to bring the Gillioz, and the rest of downtown, back to life.

8. The Reopening

Here's a happy ending—or, better yet, a new beginning. Let's call it a clear, cool late afternoon in October 2006, when downtown Springfield hums with activity. Strolling the car-lined streets, some are just finished browsing the specialty shops lining South Avenue. Some have enjoyed a specialty coffee in a mudhouse that carries their favorite specialty magazine. Some are thinking hard about dinner somewhere on Walnut Street, trying to decide which specialty cuisine suits their palates. Some can't wait for nighttime, when their favorite local band plays at their favorite specialty nightclub where they will drink their favorite specialty drink. Specialties, indeed: in offering "an alternative to the franchise culture," to "the prefabricated thing where everything is predictable" (Keyes), the downtown shops will have to specialize, be a little more creative, a little more precious. Whereas the nation's indoor air-conditioned suburban mega-malls are made for "power-shopping," as the phrase goes, the downtown's specialty shops are made for strolling and for sitting, for sipping, for luxuriating over conversation, for people-watching. These are the urban-cultural "fine arts" that suburban malls don't

Restored Marquee, "Thanks Springfield."

Restoration in Progress. Marquee.

to life, which has allowed urban culture to reassert itself and stand as an equal (or near-equal) economic partner with suburban culture and its mega-malls. And, as we've hinted above, urban culture's advantage over suburban culture is primarily aesthetic. The suburbs have their distinctive forms of entertainment, their country clubs and golf courses and multiplex cinemas; Hollywood, indeed, plays in the suburbs. But along with its specialty-shopping, the city is once again the center of live-variety entertainment. Live theater, live dance, live music, both high-brow and low-brow: these are distinctively, quintessentially urban expressions. (The ballet does not play at the mall.)

While the downtown remains "historic," its history alone could not have saved it. "Let's face the facts," said architect Tim Rosenbury in the March 9, 2003 *News-Leader:* "Things have changed, and for us to be nostalgic about down-town is to not give down-

always cultivate. Whatever a suburban mega-mall can't (or won't, or shouldn't) hold will likely be found downtown. Antique stores don't belong in malls; purveyors of the used and past, they'll be welcomed downtown. If it isn't new and can't be sold in volume, then it probably won't be sold at a mall; but it will likely be sold downtown, where shoppers come for surprises. If it's not a first-run hit Hollywood action movie, then it won't show at a suburban multiplex cinema; but it will likely show at a small downtown house specializing in foreign- and art-films. There are no museums in malls and few private galleries; "mall art" (if such exists) is mass-produced. If you want an original piece signed by the artist, you'll go downtown.

We do not write this as a critique of suburbia; heaven knows we've all cheerfully spent our dollars in its malls. Our point is that Springfield, like other cities nationwide, has apparently completed its latest demographic shift. No longer simply emptying itself into the suburbs, the city (that is, the historic downtown) has come back

town a chance.... The old wine is gone, and the incredible challenge is putting new wine in these old wine skins" (Keyes 1A). The clock, simply, cannot be run back. Yet the Gillioz is precisely one of those "old wine skins" into which "new wine" has been poured. The aim of the theater's restoration is not nostalgia per se; if it were, then the restored Gillioz would become a museum and not a living, functional theater with genuine prospects for profits. Into this revitalized urban setting, then, where novelty and specialty reign supreme, the Gillioz Theatre Beautiful takes its encore, reclaiming its status as the city's grand palace. Its re-emergence from layers of dirt, decay, and neglect has been a long time coming, requiring millions of dollars and a seemingly equal number of man-hours. Like any master work, the Gillioz couldn't be rebuilt in a day; in the beginning, its would-be artists didn't even have a whole canvas to work on.

In 1987, Jim D. Morris succeeded where M. E. Gillioz had failed: acting on a tip from Sam Freeman, Morris managed to purchase the theater's St. Louis Street store-

Restoration in Progress. Doors.

front. Until then, the property's hundred-year lease had thwarted would-be developers. Listing the Gillioz on the National Register of Historic Places was crucial for fund-ing, yet the nomination could not proceed until the Gil-lioz properties were united. Acquiring the auditorium in 1990, Morris joined other local philanthropists in a non-

Restoration in Progress. Mezzanine.

Restoration in Progress. Mezzanine hall.

profit organization that would spearhead the theater's listing on the National Register and, ultimately, its restoration. In 1991 the Springfield Landmarks Preservation Trust was formed. That same year the Gillioz won its rightful place on the National Register. On October 27, 1992, Morris graciously deeded the theater to the Trust. The Gillioz Theatre Project had begun.

Still, funding remained a challenge. After all, the bill for restoration had reached an estimated $7 million, $4 million of which would be generated through donations and $3 million through grants and tax credit programs (Hocklander, "Backers" 17L). Funding first came from the municipal government and through the Neighborhood Assistance Program, which provided "state tax credits [for] in-kind contributions of labor and material" (McCann 26). Slowly the Trust's vision was turning to reality. In 1995 the city made loans available to face-lift the façades of buildings downtown. By means of this loan program and a generous donation by Missouri Neon, a new three-sided marquee—a near-replica of the original—was installed, making for a marvelous seventieth birthday celebration in 1996. (See figure: Restored Marquee, "Thanks Springfield.")

The vision sharpened further in 1998, when the Trust acquired the old Netter's Building next door (Hocklander, "Backers" 17L). Renamed the Jim D. Morris Arts Building, its leasing to retailers would provide further

financial support for the Gillioz. Renovation of this second building added $1.5 million to the project's total cost. Fortunately, the Preservation Trust had found generous sources of additional funding: the Missouri Department of Natural Resources, the Springfield-Greene County Historic Preservation Society, and the Community Foundation of the Ozarks.

For all its neglect the Gillioz was still "in incredible shape" (Hocklander, "Backers" 17L): so noted the restoration's head architect, Craig Hacker of Butler, Rosenbury and Associates. Still the roof, windows, and exterior brick needed repair and the building needed to be brought up to code. An army of contractors came to the rescue: Norm Goth of Smith Goth Engineers, David Peerbolte of Peerbolte Consulting, Elise Crane (project manager) and Darrell Montgomery (job superintendent) of DeWitt and Associates. At a cost of $500,000 a City Utilities substation was installed in the basement.

Next in line was the theater's finery. Gunar Gruenke of Conrad Schmitt Studios (the firm responsible for such restoration projects as Union Station in St. Louis and the Waldorf-Astoria in New York City) subcontracted with the Chicago-based Luczak Brothers to restore the interior walls and surface ornaments. Once the plaster work was repaired, layers of paint were stripped off and the original colors analyzed, so they could be replicated with precision. (See figures: Restoration in Progress.)

Now the movie house had to be put back together, since its old owner, Dickinson Theatres, had sold off the usable projection equipment, screen, and organ. A Trust board member, Nancy Brown Dornan, turned to Dickinson Theatres and its area manager, Bill Burnett, who happened to have been the Gillioz Theatre's last manager and had a soft spot still for the old Theatre Beautiful. She hoped that Burnett could provide the screen that once hung in Battlefield Mall's Century 21 (an ironic twist, since the Century 21 had contributed to the Gillioz Theatre's demise). More than a screen, Burnett gave Dornan some curious news. In the basement of the Tower Theatre (also a Dickinson property) some of the Gillioz Theatre's original furniture had been kept in storage. Sure enough, a love seat, settee, two matching chairs, and a mirror were recovered from the Tower and moved to the Jim D. Morris Arts Building for safekeeping.

Unfortunately, someone else took a liking to the furniture and it was stolen out of the Morris Building. The furniture was discovered missing on May 29, 2003, and on June 6 the *Springfield News-Leader* reported the theft. Amazingly on June 8, just two days after the *News-Leader* article, Southwest Missouri State University security officers discovered the furniture at the top of the campus parking garage on Cherry Street (Hocklander, "Gillioz" 1B). The Springfield Police picked up the furniture and stored it for nine months before anyone on the Trust board knew of its recovery. (The sequence, then: furniture lost, furniture found; furniture lost again, furniture found.)

The original seats had also been lost. In the early 1980s a developer had high hopes of restoring the theater. The original seats were bare wood, though upholstered cushions had been added in the 1930s. As part of his own restoration work, he had them removed from the theater and stripped off the upholstery. Yet he soon went bankrupt and his warehouses (with the seats in storage) were sold off. The warehouses then passed through several hands, with no one quite aware of their historic contents. Through a stroke of luck the seats were eventually identified and returned to the Gillioz. (Again, furniture lost, furniture found.) Refinished by a company in California, they will find their way back into the restored theater.

Remarkably, the theater's terra-cotta façade, French doors, and stained-glass "signature G" window have survived intact. Originally, the marquee had a high vertical sign above it, though the restored front does not. The original ticket booth was positioned in the middle of the entrance bay (tellers had to lock themselves in while selling tickets); unfortunately, the booth no longer survives. In its place a modernized box office has been cut into the outer lobby's west wall, which tellers will access through the Morris Building.

When finished, the interior will look dazzling—just as it did on the theater's opening night, though the technology will have changed. The projection room will be

Restoration in Progress. Rotunda.

Restoration in Progress. East arcade.

Restoration in Progress. Scaffolding.

Restoration in Progress. Decorative elements.

field Landmarks Preservation Trust announced that the Jim D. Morris Arts Building and the Gillioz Theatre would be named the Ronald and Nancy Reagan Center. The naming was, of course, in honor of the actor and president; but the naming also acknowledged Ronald Reagan as the theater's benefactor—as its patron saint if you will, whose historic connection with the Gillioz stage has helped fund the theater's restoration. As Representative Blunt so eloquently put it, "Having President Reagan's name on this complex reflects a unique moment in Springfield's history and is a fitting tribute to President Reagan's service to the nation, his contribution to the arts, the movie industry and his ties to the Gillioz Theatre." It is also fitting that the Gillioz, in all its refurbished glory, should become the jewel in the crown of a revitalized downtown.

In the March 10, 2003 *News-Leader,* a onetime resident expressed surprise upon learning that friends had moved back to the old city center. "Why would anyone want to live in the warehouse-and-wino part of town?" she asked

outfitted with new projectors, a mixing board and sound system. Dan Chilton of the Moxie Cinema, John Gott of SLS Sound Systems, Bob Heil of Heil Sounds, Mike Scott of Springfield's KY3 Television, and Dave Wilson of Sounds Great Productions will have helped by donating and installing lighting, television production cables, and the latest sound and recording equipment.

On June 7, 2002—the fiftieth anniversary of *The Winning Team* and its Springfield premiere—Nancy Reagan "accepted a position as member of the Gillioz Theatre Honorary Board." Southwest Missouri Congressman Roy Blunt was instrumental in arranging for her gracious acceptance and he has been instrumental since in securing federal funding (totaling $1 million to date) on the theater's behalf. It was the theater's historic connection to the Reagans that made such legislation and funding possible. What could be more fitting, then, than to name the combined Gillioz and Morris buildings after the most famous couple ever to grace the Gillioz stage? On July 31, 2004, Representative Blunt and the Spring-

(Hocklander, "Arts" 5A). Of course, she "hadn't seen Springfield in 20 years." When she next comes to town, we hope she visits the Ronald and Nancy Reagan Center and its restored Gillioz.

1931 Little Miss Springfield.

9. Springfield Remembers the Gillioz

In an ad celebrating its first anniversary, the Gillioz management addressed a letter "To Mr. and Mrs. Springfield:"

> We appreciate, to the fullest extent, the generous patronage that has made it possible for us to give to the public the highest type of entertainment....
>
> The Gillioz Theater serves two purposes. First, to make Springfield proud of it; second, to serve the public. The Gillioz, without undue modesty, is proud of itself. Proud of its dazzling splendor, proud of its affiliations to secure the finest pictures and stage attractions. Proud to be located in Springfield, but proudest of all when Springfield is proud of it.
>
> The Management

As the following reminiscences suggest, the city of Springfield is indeed proud of its new-old theater. We have sorted the memories thematically: children first, then workers, then sweethearts. For good measure, we end with a few mystery sightings.

Children

Marimartha Ritter remembers riding with her father, Paul Roper—owner of Roper's Store in West Plains—when he would drive to Springfield for merchandise. She and her future husband, Jim Ritter, attended State Teacher's College in the 1940s. She says, "I wish I could go back to the Gillioz and have it feel just like it did when I was a little girl and Daddy used to take me there. And then how it felt when I was dating Jim and we went on the weekend. And again when I was a mother and took my children. It is a very special place to me."

In 1931, when she was five years old, **Joyce (Gregg) Hunt**—"the Shirley Temple of the Ozarks," as she was called back then—was named "Little Miss Springfield." During one of her performances—Joyce danced at the Gillioz Theatre in Monett as well as in Springfield—she got to entertain "Elvira" Weaver, who was in the audi-

ence. Soon after, little Joyce entered an M.G.M. talent search, becoming a finalist: "from over a thousand contestants four children, one of which was me, were selected" for a screen test, which later showed at the Gillioz. (See figure: 1931 Little Miss Springfield.)

The youngest family member of the famous vaudeville act, the Weaver Brothers and Elviry, **Mary Weaver Sweeney** recalls making *Swing Your Lady*. She was a child on the Hollywood set with a young Ronald Reagan, who was wearing thick glasses. Later he was not wearing them and tripped over a cable, falling to the floor. When Mary laughed, her father made her apologize to Mr. Reagan. He accepted her apology, saying, "It's okay, honey, I did look pretty funny taking the tumble, I'm sure."

Villa Ann Bilyeu never missed the Weaver Brothers and Elviry when they were playing in town. As a child, Villa Ann's future husband, Freeman Glenn, sold his pet groundhog to the Weavers for use in their vaudeville show. This was during the Depression and the animal brought him $1.00. Freeman missed his groundhog, but it went on to live a life of show business! (See insert: Earl and Little Villa Ann Ride in from the Country.)

Betty (Proctor) Baker remembers dressing up on Saturdays to go to the movies. This was during the late Depression, when cars were scarce. Since her father was a bus driver, she would ride the bus downtown. She and a friend would first visit Woolworth's (on the Square's southwest corner) for a lunch of tuna fish sandwiches, potato chips, and limeade. Then the two girls would buy their movie tickets. As Betty was still months away from being twelve years old, she purchased a children's ticket (only twenty five-cents). The manager, however, whom Betty describes as being tall with curly, dark hair, didn't believe Betty was that young. Every week he would ask her to open her mouth, checking for her twelve-year molars. When Betty did turn twelve, she marched up to the manager, informing him that she would be buying her last movie ticket at children's price.

Mary Maddux remembers attending the 1952 premiere of *The Winning Team:* "Ronald Reagan was here, but not Doris Day, his co-star. Backstage, before the film, there was a crowd around Mr. Reagan. Mr. Hunter asked me, 'Would you like his autograph?' I said. 'Sure.' So he thrust a paper toward Mr. Reagan and said, 'Would you give this little lady your autograph?'"

As a child, **Robert Gibbons** also met Mr. Reagan: "I attended the premiere at the Gillioz. On stage, dancers Gene Nelson and Virginia Gibson performed and special guests Nancy Davis and Mrs. Grover Cleveland Alexander were introduced to the audience. I got Ronald Reagan's autograph, but my mother ran it through the washer in my Cub Scout uniform!"

Paula England remembers her favorite Gillioz movies, as well as her favorite theater candy: "Our family lived in West Plains during the 1950s and my grandfather always took me to Springfield to see Disney movies. It was too expensive for the theater there to get these movies. I always had Jujubes. As a child, this is what always excited me most."

Dana Gray visited the Gillioz in the mid-1960s: "It was a whole other world. I remember the drapes, carpeting, and décor. I took my children to the Gillioz. I have such fun memories."

As a six-year old, **David Coonrod** went downtown with his dad "to catch a film, *Guy's Night Out*," a fitting movie for their own father-son outing. He remembers "the grand lobby, watching movies like *The Longest Day*, *PT109*, and *Knights of the Round Table*. We both liked gladiator movies."

Robert Gibbons recalls the Wurlitzer: "During the Sixties I went to Drury with a member of the American Guild of Organists in St. Louis named Steve Schneiders. We asked the manager, Mr. Lewis, if we could come down and look at the organ. Someone had moved the console to the side and had cut the main electric cable from the console to the pipes! We managed to splice enough wires back for Steve to play the organ."

At Work

A cashier at the Gillioz in the 1930s, **Francis Hardy Gibbons** tells of families "coming in to the theater on hot days, spending the day in the cool air and leaving corn cobs and chicken bones from their picnic lunches. People would go in there and literally stay all day." (**Steve Barry** also remembers "when two movies ran all day. There was no air-conditioner at home, so my family took a picnic lunch and went to the balcony and spread a blanket. We watched the movies until it cooled off at night and went home.") (See insert: Robbery at the Gillioz!)

Mr. Kerkemeyer, whose barbershop lay across the street, remembers a hot summer day at the Gillioz when "the air conditioner

Earl and Little Villa Ann Ride in from the Country. Earl Bilyeu, Jr. remembers climbing up into the bed of his family's old pick-up truck with his sister, little Villa Ann, anticipating the long trip from Spokane, Missouri, to Springfield. Earl can still feel each bump in the winding dirt road. Sheltering from the dust that wouldn't let up until his family reaches paved road in Ozark, he clings to his only protection, the ragged tarp that his father had thrown over him and his brothers and sisters. Peeking occasionally out from underneath, Earl spots the familiar elm trees lining National Avenue, forming a canopy of leaves overhead. The elms tell Earl that he is now finally, officially in Springfield and nearer to the highlight of his trip: after their father's business and mother's shopping, their day will end with a movie at the Gillioz. In the meantime, he day-dreams of buttered popcorn, whose smell "fills the Gillioz's lobby and auditorium," and the feel of carpeting under his feet—"a rarity in the Ozarks," Earl notes, "unless you went to one of the nicer hotels like the Kentwood or the Colonial."

For her part, little Villa Ann imagines herself in one of the theater's newly-upholstered seats, worrying only that an usher might lead in one of those high-heeled Springfield women, who "always dress up in hats and gloves," seating her right in front. Then she'd be stuck behind "a fancy hat and wouldn't be able to see the screen." At least she can count on a spotless theater, since the "white-haired Black gentleman who keeps the theater clean wouldn't allow so much as a piece of popcorn to stay on the floor for very long." Villa Ann can't wait to see the cartoon but she knows she'll first have to endure a newsreel or two, or three.

wasn't working quite right." He had just purchased two pairs of tan suit pants for $25.50. Taking a siesta from his own sweaty business, he sat down on one of the theater's cushioned seats and, when he got up afterward, his new pants were stained red! He didn't tell the manager. It took him several washes to get the stain out.

While in high school in the Fifties, **Betty Davis** worked as an usherette: "As I recall, it was quite a prestigious job, one where you could see all your friends when they came to the movies and you could see all the first-run movies free (over and over and over)! As if that wasn't enticement enough, a grey satin uniform was provided. In fact, the job was such a plum that I gave up a fifty cents-an-hour job at Evans Drug Store to take the Gillioz job for thirty-five cents an hour." Ms. Davis worked the night of *The Winning Team* premiere.

Jean Coberl remembers working "at the Gillioz for Tindell Lewis. He hired me away from Robert's Meat Market—my father's business—when I was bringing him some hot dogs that he had bought.... I remember when popcorn sold for fifteen, then twenty-five, then fifty cents. Even then, you received change back from $1.00 at the concession stand. I remember *Hawaii*, with Julie Andrews and Richard Harris." (See figure: Gillioz Concession Booth, 1940s.)

When Carol Burnett worked at the Fox Theater, "Mr. George Hunter," who was the District Manager at the time, "would send me down to the Gillioz to help Mr.

Robbery at the Gillioz! The March 20, 1933 *Kansas City Star* reports: "Two bandits entered the Fox-Gillioz theater this morning, obtained an estimated $300 in cash and left the manager, Jack Moore, bound."

Lewis when he was short-handed. One of my favorite shows at the Gillioz was *Wine and Roses* with Jack Lemmon…. It was such a wonderful emotional picture. There wasn't a dry eye anywhere as people left the theater."

While cleaning up as a janitor, **Jim Wunderle** remembers finding "purses, wallets, gloves, coats, the occasional one shoe. I found a plastic case containing bullets after the vice squad had been there checking out" one of the adult movies then showing. "The all time weirdest thing," in his opinion, was "a baggie containing small boiled potatoes."

Robert E. Bretcher worked at the Gillioz when the theater closed: "On Tuesday July 15, 1980, yours truly ran the last 35mm movie there. It was *The Amityville Horror*, with James Brolin and Margot Kidder. As I threaded the last reel of the last show, I said to myself, 'This is truly a sad day. I really hope it isn't the end of the theater.'"

At Play

Jean Etta Brown went to the Gillioz during World War II while attending Drury College: "I remember before the movie started there was an organ player and a beautiful young singer named Marilyn Jorgenson. The song I remember she sang so often was,

> I love life and I just want to live,
> Drink of life's fullness,
> Take all it can give.
> I love life, every moment must count,
> I glory in its sunshine
> And revel in its fount!

This is a fond memory for me."

"The Gillioz Theatre," says **Sally Chowning**, "is where my husband and I went on our first date in 1963. We saw a movie called *Spencer's Mountain*. Coincidentally, I saw part of the movie being filmed the summer I worked in Yellowstone National Park." (See insert: College Students Out and About Town.)

Eugene Richards recalls the local protests surrounding Richard Burton and Elizabeth Taylor's 1966 film, *Who's Afraid of Virginia Woolf?* "I remember going down to St. Louis street to see what was going on. There were people everywhere protesting the movie. I decided myself to see what the movie was all about, so I broke the picket line and went and saw *Virginia Woolf*. I didn't like the movie, but stayed and watched the whole thing."

In 2003 the Springfield Landmarks Preservation Trust received the following note, accompanied by a check: "In the spring of 1968, **Bob Lummis** and **Patsy Graves** went to the Gillioz Theatre to see the movie, *The Graduate*. It was their first date. Please accept the enclosed donation from their family in honor of their 35th wedding anniversary, which they celebrated September 28th."

Jim Wunderle met his wife at the theater: "I started working there in 1976 and she started out selling popcorn. And we're still together."

Mystery Sightings!

There's been a lot spoken about **Elvis Presley's visit to the Gillioz** while he was in town on May 16, 1956, performing that evening at the Shrine Mosque. Most Springfieldians have heard the story once or twice. To set the record straight, we quote from a recent *News-Leader* article:

> Elvis' attempt to find a bit of peace and quiet away from [his] grueling schedule caused a minor panic. **Les Reynolds,** then a Springfield police officer assigned to security at the Mosque, recalls that Elvis' manager, "Colonel" Tom Parker, discovered his star missing in late afternoon.
>
> "He asked me where was the nearest theater,"

College Students Out and About Town. In its "About Town" column, the March 3, 1937 *Kansas City Star* reports: "Margaret Lucas [of] Crane, Mo., tells of two college boys, slightly the worse for wear, who, entering the lobby of the Gillioz theater in Springfield, grinned amorously at an attractive girl standing there.

'Oafs!' she commented, drawing herself up with an icy stare.

'Oh, gosh, Bill!' one of the lads remarked to the other, 'She works crossword puzzles, too!'"

says Reynolds. "I told him the Gillioz was a couple of blocks down the street. We got a patrol car to give 'the colonel' a ride there to look for Elvis."

Sure enough, Elvis was located in the Gillioz watching *Jubal*, a western starring Glenn Ford. (O'Brien, "Local Lucky Fans" 1C, 4C)

To be precise, Elvis was seen sitting in the back, in the first seat to the right of the last row down the west aisle on the first floor. "Colonel" Parker knew Elvis's fondness for movies, and could lay odds where to find him.

Robert Gibbons remembers the event slightly differently: "I remember my mother wouldn't let me go. I was ten or eleven. We drove by [the Shrine Mosque] and there were all these girls hanging off the fire escapes trying to get a glimpse of Elvis. Les Reynolds was to take care of Elvis, but he's looking around and doesn't see Elvis. So they sent three policemen, one to the Gillioz, one to the Jewell, and one to the Landers. I heard Elvis walked down Main Street, paid his admission. The cashier didn't recognize him."

Another reputed sighting is worth mentioning: **the Gillioz ghost.** (Every theater is supposed to have one, right?) The debate as to whether the Gillioz is haunted continues to rage. Here, both sides give their account of what "really" happens after the lights turn out.

Jim Wunderle doesn't believe there's a ghost: "The

Gillioz Concession Booth, 1940s.

that the movie stopped. We know that the audience began to complain, which brought the manager out of his office to investigate. And we know that the manager, shoving the door open, found the projectionist lying dead on the floor. What happened afterward remains a bit murky.

In the version that sifted its way down to Ellison, the manager stepped over the projectionist, restarted the film—the show must go on!—and then went downstairs to call for an ambulance. When the ambulance men arrived, they climbed the stairs and carried the man's body back down, the audience remaining blissfully unaware of the proceedings.

Robert Gibbons heard a somewhat more colorful version from his uncle, Elmer Nuttlemann, who worked part-time at the theater as a projectionist. Uncle Elmer told him that a Bridgette Bardot movie was playing, and that the film came off track "at a crucial time in the plot, when Bardot was taking off her towel." The men in the audience began complaining loudly, bringing the manager, Mr. Lewis, out of his office. He discovered the projectionist dead on the booth floor, but he didn't restart the film. Not that he didn't know how. He wasn't allowed. The projectionist was a union job and it was a strong union, so even Mr. Lewis dared not restart the film. He had to call the union office and request a replacement projectionist, who came and restarted the film. "The audience about rioted until the film got going again," Gibbons adds. (His uncle didn't say whom Mr. Lewis called first: the union office or the ambulance.)

story was that some patron had passed away there in the Thirties and still haunted the place. One rather eccentric box office gal claimed to have seen him. I can say without a doubt it just ain't so. I was there at every hour of the day and night. Sometimes I'd go down to clean at 2:00 a.m. It was spooky. No ghosts, though, and I was open to seeing one. I'd take a break and fire up the 'Mighty Wurlitzer.' ... Some nights I felt like the Phantom of the Opera."

Sam Freeman begs to differ. One night while preparing for a theater fund raiser he left to get something to eat, at which time the stage curtain was down. When he returned an hour later, the curtain was up! It had not been used for years and it would have been hard for anyone to raise; besides, no one else was there to raise it. Freeman believes it was the spirit of the Gillioz ghost preparing for another show.

Gary Ellison also believes that something mysterious goes on: "Nancy [Brown Dornan] and I were in the theater during the late afternoon to make sure everything was ready for a First Night, New Year's Eve tour. We went home for dinner and returned around 6:30 p.m. When we got back, we saw that the asbestos fire curtain had been lowered about half way down, revealing a big 'G' emblem painted on it. For all the time we had spent in the theater, we had never seen this before. Neither of us knew that the fire curtain still existed, let alone had the 'G' on it. And no one else had been in the theater. We joked that the Gillioz ghost wanted the First Night visitors to see something special" that evening.

We cannot confirm that a patron died in the Thirties, though a projectionist did pass away in the call of duty. We know for a fact that he was shut up in his hot projection booth, behind the steel door. We know that the only reason anyone knew something had happened was

Could the projectionist's spirit live on in the Gillioz? Or could the Gillioz ghost be that star-crossed lover who wrote the letters found in the same projection room?

During the theater's restoration a stack of letters from the 1930s was found in the booth, hidden in a wall. Postmarked from Billings, Missouri, they were apparently written by a single mother to a married man in Springfield. How scandalous this affair would have been during the Depression! She writes, "No one else looks at it as we do of course, but there is only Us so I don't give a hoot what they say." Her devotion to the man goes beyond all reason: "You're the only thing in life I want," she writes, adding, "Why must I do my duty to these kids when my whole being is spent adoring you?" Dramatic!

The woman writes not only of her passion but of her hardships. In one letter she tells her lover that she must get a factory job making dresses, so she can pay the bills. She writes, "The wages are $8 for 32 ½ hours. That means 63 hours in two weeks. Lover it's easy work and not to be sneezed at. But to you who makes more every week than I shall in a month it's probably insignificant. It means the difference right now between starvation and luxury to me." Who was she, then? Why were her letters hidden in the wall? Her lover was apparently a projectionist. Why didn't he destroy them? (He was married, after all: this much the letters make clear.)

So much about the letters—indeed, so much about the Gillioz—remains a mystery. There they were, the records of a passionate, clandestine affair, tucked away in the highest, brightest, most stifling room of the building—the projection room, out of which streamed a brilliant eye beam, source of the theater's fantasy-images. How much life has been lived there, secreted away in that room? How much dreaming? Behind what other wall, beside which seat, in what corner of the balcony, near which railing were other lives lived, other secrets kept? The mystery of the Gillioz remains wrapped up in the untold stories of those unnamed others who worked there, played there, loved there, laughed there, cried there; yes, one or perhaps two died there. More than Elvis, it is the mysterious woman of the letters whose spirit we should seek to glimpse in the foyer, the balcony, backstage; her very anonymity expresses the way most of the theater's visitors lived out their lives. But to live life against the backdrop of such a grand theater: that is a splendid thing, indeed.

Our mystery woman wrote a poem. Like a message in a bottle, it resurfaced with her letters. An English professor is not likely to give it high marks. Still, she did her best and it's worth a read. In high, Hollywood fashion, let's pretend that she writes to the Gillioz, that her love affair is with the theater. (Why not? The movies teach us poetic licence.) Read this way, the poem sums up not an anonymous individual's but a community's love affair with life and its memories, its aspirations, its dreaming—and with the theater where this living, this dreaming took place:

Possession

Dear Love you are the world and all to me.
The wonder of it all lies on my heart.
I marvel that we lived before we met,
For each of us is of the other a big part.

You are the dearest thing that ever happened,
You're all my dreams and wishes Dear come
                                                         true,
You are my Prince in all his shining armor,
You wonder that my heart belongs to you.

Dear heart you've earned each thing I've ever given,
For all your dearness I can never pay.
Yet each thing I have done was freely given:
I love you Dear — what more is there to say?

I'm not blind to all your faults, Dear:
I see them just as plain as you see mine.
Yet all you do for me does but outshine them,
For I belong to you and you are mine.

I love you — first, last and always with all my heart forever.

As they say in Hollywood:

The end.

How to Enter Vaudeville.

Coda:
Vaudeville/Ozarks/America

I don't have a very quick sense of humor. Half of the great comedians I've had in my shows and that I paid a lot of money to and who made my customers shriek were not only not funny to me, but I couldn't understand why they were funny to anybody. You'd be surprised how many of the expensive comics I've run out on and locked myself in my office when they were on stage.

—Florence Ziegfield

What was his touch? ... First, Ziegfield knew the subtle line between desire and lust, between good taste and vulgarity, and never crossed it. He came close a few times but he never quite crossed it. Second, the exhibitionism which was part of his private life was not contrived. It was an integral part of him, part of the personality mechanism that made him what he was: a gambler who had an almost childish irresponsibility toward the value of money and an equally childish conviction that he could always get some more when he wanted it. Most of the time he was astonishingly right. And finally, he had a sense of showmanship and of female beauty that was the despair of his competitors.

—Marjorie Farnsworth

There was one badge of honor worn by all these performers. It was the simple but proud statement, "I worked for Ziegfeld."

—Will Rogers

Writing in the November 1922 issue of *New Republic*, Mary Cass Canfield rhapsodizes over the technical and artistic virtuosity, variety, and magnificence—in sum, the "perfection" —of Mr. Florence Ziegfield's Follies:

Vaudeville is happy; therefore it is both good and beautiful. Laughter preaches fellowship better than sermons; enjoyment throws magic loveliness, a golden glow, over a bare stage where a comedian in a check suit gregariously leans against a backdrop lamp post.... No song or dance or comic skit is too long; brevity, queen of qualities, smiles triumphantly out at us between the quiet rises and falls of innumerable, fantastically colored curtains. Vaudeville leads us, breathlessly but interested, from acrobats to sentimental songs, from pony ballets to well-played one-act tragedy. Every musician in the orchestra is mentally on his toes, every pulley is super-greased. To concentrate on the stage management of the Follies is like watching a thoroughbred take a series of fences. The revolving stage has a soul, it bounds forward to its task with swagger, it prides itself on never making a mistake. It is American. (S224)

American, indeed: if jazz was America's great musical invention, then vaudeville was its theater. (See figure: *How to Enter Vaudeville.*) "For all its similarity with European entertainments, vaudeville was a uniquely American achievement and fulfilled uniquely American needs" (M6), writes Albert F. McLean in his *American Vaudeville as Ritual.* As a coda to Springfield's by no means unique theater history, we might consider McLean's list of such "uniquely American needs." As a social critic, McLean is occasionally hard-nosed in his arguments; we needn't agree with him in every respect, though his arguments are worth noting.

First, vaudeville grew in response to the nation's own urban growth. While the circus, minstrel shows, medicine shows, and other popular entertainments of the late nineteenth century reflected largely rural values, prejudices, and tastes, vaudeville was quintessentially an entertainment of and for the city, for "it was the nature of the city itself that novelty, variety, and a quick succession of images on stage should express its complexity and constant motion" (M7). Indeed, vaudeville "provided that esthetic encounter that ... rural segments of the population longed to make with the urban civilization that was absorbing them" (M11). It hardly surprises, then, that the Gillioz, like other theaters, would locate downtown "where communal life was its most active and where all elements of society were most likely to mingle" (M34).

Second, unlike high-brow opera and low-brow burlesque, vaudeville appealed to the nation's ascendant middle class, with its "steadily increasing affluence, its appetite for consumer goods, its ambitions for its children, and its awed envy of the wealthy and socially prominent." Through early decades of the twentieth century, "this new white-collar class was groping for an identity, seeking to make known to the patricians above and to the labourers beneath—as well as to itself—its common interests and motivation." Vaudeville would give shape to this white-collar class-identity by providing "a community of feeling and a sense of importance ... topics of conversation, sexual stimulation, memories, standards of taste, and a tangible presence located so centrally in the city that no one might overlook it" (M42).

Third, the vaudeville theaters, circuits, and star system all played to the American Dream, that Horatio Alger mythos of entrepreneurial success:

> ... as crude and vulgar as the ritual manifestation of the Myth of Success may have seemed to some observers, it was a powerful molder of the American way of life and was a foundation upon which other entertainment empires were to rise. The vaudeville palaces were not aberrations on the American scene, nor did they speak merely to the bold, the crass, the neurotic, or the alienated. Within the walls of these palaces gathered the hardworking and respectable members of society as well, caught up in the tinsel ... largely unaware that their world was being reshaped and revalued before their very eyes. (M15)

The Gillioz Theatre's lofty, gilded auditorium elicits the sort of hushed wonder once reserved for Europe's royal palaces and Baroque cathedrals. Yet vaudeville's secular idols were, again, uniquely American: rugged individualism, self-assertion and self-reliance, immense wealth, Promethean technology, progress, innovation, and modernity. Newness, indeed, and youthfulness permeated the spirit of 1920s America, distinguishing our nation from its war-weary European forebears. Separated from their (mostly European) cultural roots, Americans were free to re-invent themselves heroically—and myth-making was the stuff of the American entertainment industry.

Europe's aristocratic palaces and buildings of State remained closed and aloof to its common people; yet these same people, arriving as immigrants in America, found such palaces replicated in theaters that welcomed their presence and cheerfully received their money. As McLean argues,

> To the immigrant the spiritual promise of his religion had been manifest in the hues, lines, and lights of the cathedrals, and when he came to the United States, he could not help seeing the symbolic promise—not for the life hereafter but for the present life—in the vaudeville palaces. By its proportions and decor the vaudeville palace made easier the immigrant's translation from the rites of a ceremonial religion to the ritual of secular amusement. (M195)

We don't disparage the faith to which immigrants clung upon arriving in the America; perhaps McLean overstates this last point, though (as we noted earlier) Springfield's own Ministerial Alliance did struggle to keep its congregations in church on Sundays and out of the theaters. Still, McLean makes an intriguing observation regarding such theaters' symbolic "proportions and decor." The parish church, the city hall, the high school: in a typical town, these would be the largest, most expensive, most important public buildings, the focal points of communal life and the loci of religious, legal, civic authority. To this short list, American cities of the early twentieth century would have added—the theater. (The evidence of one's eyes confirms that, even today, no church in Springfield—nor any other theater or public building, for that matter—rivals the restored Gillioz in lavish, gold-gilt ornamentation. It doesn't surprise that the Gillioz Theatre's onetime downtown rival, the Electric, has become a church building; nor does it surprise that several of the city's vacated churches have been converted to theaters: such is a common, happy ending for old churches and old theaters alike.)

Finally, vaudeville's theaters and entertainments helped turn a nation of immigrants into a nation of Americans. True, the characterizations of vaudeville proceeded by way of stereotype. In his 1925 essay, "The Vaudeville Philosopher," Marshall D. Beuick complains of the "standard subjects that are used almost every night on the vaudeville stages throughout the country":

> An audience, composed of many persons mentally fatigued after a day's work, learns a philosophy that embraces such precepts as: marriage is an unfortunate institution to which the majority of us resign ourselves; women are fashion-crazy, spend money heedlessly and believe that their husbands are fools; politics is all bunk; prohibition should be prohibited; mothers are the finest persons in the world ... next to grandmothers; fathers are unfortunate persons upon whom fall most of life's woes; marital infidelity is widespread; clandestine affairs of most any sort between at least one married person and another of the opposite sex are comical; and finally "nothing in life really matters. The main thing to do is to get all the money you can and keep your mother-in-law as far off as possible." (S227)

Arguably, though, the predominance of stereotypes—particularly the variety of ethnic types pervading its comedy: the bumbling German professor, the parsimonious Scotsman, the drunken Irish laborer, and so on—created a sense of equality, of belonging among the theater's (that is, the city's) own ethnically, culturally, religiously diverse audiences. At home in an audience of immigrants, one laughed along with other immigrants at the foibles (however stereotyped) of one's ethnic neighbors. Such character-types trod Springfield's vaudeville stages, introducing themselves to a city still predominantly Scotch-Irish in ancestry. For its part, Springfield sent its own ethnic type—most famously, the Weaver Brothers' hillbilly "Arkansaw Travelers," Abner and Cicero—to palaces nation- and world-wide, introducing the rest of America to a little (of course, stereotyped) piece of the Ozarks. But they would tread the stage in turn: the Ozarker after the New Yorker, the Irishman, the Italian, the Jew … all, all American. Only the African American would be left off the Gillioz stage and excluded from the audience. (Of Springfield's downtown theaters, only the Landers admitted African Americans. While the others had balconies, the Landers had a second, "colored" balcony accessed by a separate side entrance and stairway. Only in the 1960s would African Americans be allowed in the Gillioz for reasons other than to clean up.)

In a sense, though, variety-vaudeville never died; its acts and its implicit values, rather, were absorbed by rival media. Thus, after its wiring for sound in 1928, the Gillioz began to show Warner Brothers' Vitaphone vaudeville reels. (Since the latest film technology allowed for singing and sound, the vaudeville show could still "go on," albeit filmed.) Radio, too, grew into an important medium of live-variety entertainment, though the most potent of all live media arrived with television. Like radios in the early 1920s, "television sets were an oddity" (R119) in the early 1950s. "Reception was poor at first" in the Ozarks, yet stores could count on "a large crowd of viewers simply by placing a set in the store window and tuning it to the station with the least-fuzzy picture" (R119). Indeed, "in Springfield the number of homes with television increased from 3% in 1953 to 95% in 1959" (R120): an astounding jump, explicable in part by the city's sudden, brief prominence in the nascent live-television industry.

KWTO's nationally-syndicated radio show, "Korn's-a-Krackin,'" had itself begun as an "unabashed hillbilly version of the popular Ole Olsen and Chic Johnson vaudeville show, Hell's-a-Poppin" (Spears-Stewart, *Remembering* 3), and "all the talent that performed on Korn's-a-Krackin' would later form the nucleus of the *Ozark Jubilee*" (Spears-Stewart, *Remembering* 3). Broadcast live from the Jewell (that is, from the old Jefferson Theatre, refurbished and reopened in 1948), Red Foley's *Ozark Jubilee* aired on KYTV. Every Saturday night from January 22, 1955 to September 24, 1960, "some 25 million television viewers from coast to coast were spellbound by the *Ozark Jubilee*" (Spears-Stewart, *Remembering* 1). Its guest performers included Eddy Arnold, Chet Atkins, Gene Autry, Pat Boone, Johnny Cash, Patsy Cline, Snooky Larson, Minnie Pearl, Jim Reeves, Tex Ritter, and Porter Wagoner. Discovered by Foley, an eleven-year-old Brenda Lee made her TV debut on the *Jubilee.*

And, thus, the city's entertainments had come full circle. Whereas the town's theaters during decades prior to World War II provided primarily city entertainment, drawing rural folks into Springfield for shopping and a night on the town, radio and television audiences nationwide looked to Springfield of the 1950s as a center of rural, folk entertainment. As a musical-cultural tourist attraction, "the Ozarks" of the 1920s remained in gestation; with the 1950s *Ozark Jubilee,* this region would burst onto the national entertainment scene, giving birth to Branson in the process. Arguably, country music couldn't become so entirely "American chic," so long as our nation hadn't yet completed its economic-demographic shift from a primarily agrarian to an urban, industrial culture. Having become a citified nation, our leisure-entertainments could now look back to "country life" and its pastimes as if to modes of pastoral escape. In sum, America would now turn to the Ozarks for its live-variety entertainments, and these would serve to connect the rest of citified-suburban America to its idealized rural past. As Ralph Foster said of the televised *Jubilee,* "there are more country people in America than any other kind. Most city folks are from the country originally and are still sentimentally attached to it" (Marymount 8D).

So, the stage curtain would again rise in Southwest Missouri. If the citified version of variety-vaudeville had slipped away, its countrified version would be reborn in Branson.

Appendices

A. Two articles (edited for readability) follow from the *Springfield Daily News*. The first, from September 18, 1909, reports on the Landers' anticipated opening; the second, from September 19, reports on the theater's first production. Given the theater's burning in 1919, the reporter was right to emphasize its fire escapes. (We might add that the Electric, too, burned in 1949.)

FINEST THEATER IN THE SOUTHWEST WILL OPEN TONIGHT

**Every Seat Taken
For First Attraction In New Landers
Two Thousand Lights To Dazzle
A Large Audience
Interior Of Playhouse
Resplendent With Gorgeous Decorations,
The Product Of The Genius
Of Best Architects**

The new Landers theater is ready for the grand and formal opening tonight. The small army of artisans, which has been engaged the past six weeks in putting the house in order, bid adieu to the finished interior this afternoon. The theater has [been] ready for the opening attraction, "The Golden Girl," for several days, and with the arrival of the company in the city today, all signs indicate a propitious bow to the public.

When the 2000 electric lights … are flashed on tonight, and with the first selection of the 11-piece orchestra, the play house will really be opened. That it will be attended by a packed house is certain, the sale of tickets having closed early in the week. Even standing room is already at a premium.

The first orchestra rehearsal in the new play house was held last night and the acoustic properties are all and more than has been expected, the softest strains of music being easily and plainly heard. Words spoken from the stage were also distinctly heard in all portions of the house....

On entering the new theater, one is conducted on the left past the box office and on the right past the elevator. Directly in front is the real opening to the parquet, which is carpeted with heavy green Brussels. On either side are broad stair cases, also carpeted with a pattern of considerable beauty, which lead to the balcony. The ladies' toilet room is on the left.... With the rays from the numerous lights scintillating over the dome, walls and balustrades, one will pause and say "exquisite," for that is the word.

The Grecian decorations and ornamental plaster effects (the latter being artistically bronzed) stud the interior and are especially numerous over and around the boxes and on the plaster beams leading to the dome....

Judging from the numerous exits afforded in the new theater, serious results in the event of a conflagration can scarcely be expected. Opening from the parquet are seven double doors which offer 14 means of escape. From the balcony, six exits lead to the ground, and from the gallery, four fire escapes offer protection.

But to the stage and the play, for "the play's the thing after all." Cutting off the stage from the balance of the house hangs a heavy asbestos curtain.... Directly to the left is the electrical apparatus faced over with the switchboard on which the controlling levers are located. The latest devices are noted and the light effects for the new Landers will be the best.

Above the stage hang numerous drop curtains and property effects which are controlled from a suspended platform by numerous ropes.

Below the stage are the dressing rooms, 16 in number. All are equipped with excellent lighting service and also have hot and cold water.... Directly in front of the stage is the orchestra pit, which is well lighted.

On the proscenium arch and also above the boxes, the letter "L" stands out in bold relief. It stands for John Landers, who has given Springfield a model, new, and up-to-date theater.

Manager Olendorf last night received a letter, the envelope of which bore the address: "George Olendorf, Manager of the Finest Theater in the Southwest, in Care of the Best City in Missouri, Springfield."

The Golden Girl Formally Opens Landers Theater
Fashionable Audience Marvels At Beauty Of Magnificent Temple Of Amusement Erected For Springfield By Well-Known Capitalist

The doors of the Landers, the magnificent new home of theatrical entertainments in Springfield, were thrown open at 7:30 o'clock last night to the smartest and most expectant audience ever assembling in Springfield.... Early in the evening Walnut street was the thoroughfare for the numerous fashionable equipages and automobiles, which conveyed the elect of Springfield society to the new theater. At the opening of the play traffic was congested by the late arrivals.

The crowd in the foyer reached its greatest proportions shortly after 8 o'clock. Until the first strains from Keet's orchestra and the rising of the first curtain on "The Golden Girl" at 8:30, a constant stream of enthusiastic and expectant humanity passed into the interior of the new play house.

It was a grand first night for the theater goers of Springfield, and they saw one of the prettiest and most modern play houses in the west, and one of the best musical productions of the day.

The new home of music, opera, drama and comedy is an architectural enterprise, the magnitude of which might well have daunted a less resolute purpose than that of the man in whose honor the theater is named, John Landers. But his success in the enterprise is the same that has characterized his business investments and propositions since a resident of this city....

"The Golden Girl," as presented by Mort Singer's splendid musical organization, was a sparkling, clean musical comedy that from the rising of the first curtain to the grand finale held the marked attention and interest of all.

The members of the cast of characters were all stars last night, but the work of Miss Marie Flynn as "Dixie Columbia Curtis," who was "The Golden Girl," was especially pleasing. A return engagement in Springfield in whatever role he may aspire of her successful suitor, Jimmy Lucas, ... will be appreciated, judging from the applause he was accorded.

Miss Mina Davis, who is a granddaughter of President Jefferson Davis of the Confederate states, as "Dorothy Hale, the fiend," was also a favorite with the audience, as was Franklin Farnum in the role of "Cadet Captain John Fisk." ...

The scene of the play is laid at West Point, and as might be supposed, a strong vein of humor runs through the entire theme. Equally as strong, however, is the pathos as presented by Charles Horn, as "General Varney," a Federal war veteran, and Peter Raymond, as "General Carroll, a Confederate veteran," and Miss Flynn.

The book and lyrics by Frank R. Adams were very clever, and the music by Joe Howard, whose catchy airs are familiar to Springfield theater goers ... excelled all previous effort.

The play takes its names from the conclusion of the second act, when, figuratively speaking, a shower of gold envelopes Miss Flynn and her chorus. Strings of tinseled effects are dropped softly from above the stage and with the added theatrical effects, a scene of surpassing beauty (the most exquisite ever presented on a Springfield stage) is gained. The scenario follows the unsuccessful attempt of "Cadet Captain Fisk" to win the hand of Miss Flynn, and who rebuffing him is transformed into a golden image.

Three curtain calls were extended by the audience.

The costumes and gowns worn by the members of the company take precedence in Springfield as being the most elaborate ever shown on a local stage and were the object of much admiration....

Manager George F. Olendorf ... was pleased with the reception accorded the new play house and the opening attraction.... To him is due considerable credit for designing the play house and all the credit for assuming the managerial role so successfully.... The opening night of the Landers will be an event long remembered in Springfield....

B. The September 9, 1911 *Springfield Leader* reported on preparations for the next day's "Big Opening" of the Jefferson. The article offers an insider's look at local stage management.

Vaudeville Artists Are Here For the Big Opening

With the arrival in Springfield of the Romano Brothers, exponents of Greek physical culture, two or three days ago, and of the Minstrel Four yesterday, things are looming up lively at the Jefferson theater ... which is to give a "first night" show at 8:30 o'clock tomorrow evening. The remainder of the members of the first week's bill are expected to come in either tonight or tomorrow and the theater will be all ready for the opening at the time specified.

The Minstrel Four has been playing as headliners of various circuits all over the country for months, and came to Springfield directly from Houston, Tex., where they were headlined on the Interstate circuit. When they conclude their engagement here they will stop at no intermediate points, but go direct to Chicago, where they will appear at the Majestic theater.

Forest Brothers, two of the four members of the troupe, are delighted with the increase in growth made by Springfield since their last visit here in 1906.... The town has grown wonderfully in the five years that have elapsed, they say, and they expressed their delight at the general prosperity and growth shown by the Queen City....

There is a lot of preliminary work connected with the opening of a theater and with its management after it is once open, and a lot of worry connected with the business that is not taken into consideration by the public before the footlights. One of the chief worries is keeping tabs on the actors, seeing that they are advertised properly before their arrival, and getting the things they will need in their acts.

About a week before the bill is changed, all of the actors who are to appear on the new bill send their photographs and advertising literature to the manager of the theater, in this case H. M. Thomas. Along with the advertising matter, the actor sends a resume to his act, together with a list of "props" or properties, the things they will need. There are a lot of articles used on the vaudeville stage that are not carried by the actors themselves, and if the theater does not have them on hand, they must be supplied from the stores about the city. When this list is properly checked off and the properties secured, there is still the worry over the possibility that the actors will be delayed in their arrival, thus cutting out at least one show. Generally there is little need in worrying along this line, but the house manager does not relax his strained expression until he has the house filled with patrons and the curtain up for the opening of the new bill.

All of the uniforms that will be worn by the employees of the Jefferson have arrived and are now in the hand of the presser in preparation for tomorrow night. The uniforms of the ushers are black with gold trimmings and are decidedly neat in appearance.

The ushers will wear little round caps bearing the word "Usher" across the band in gold letters. The stage carpenter and electrician will also have caps. Blue uniforms will be worn by the stage hands.

Gilbert Johnson will rush around behind the scenes during the acts and intermission in his capacity as stage manager and it will depend upon his efforts whether everything goes off properly behind the footlights. I. N. Williams has been secured as chief electrician and Charles Moore as the property man, in addition to which there will be a "grip," whose duty it is to raise and lower the curtain and to shift scenery. Every employee of the new Jefferson will belong to a union organization....

C. Printed in the October 10, 1916 *Springfield Republican,* the following article reports on the gala opening of the Electric. It alludes to the city's bitterly-contested streetcar strike of 1916-1917, which forced north-siders to walk downtown or else resort to the streetcars' unregulated, privately-operated rivals, the taxis and "jitneys." The twelve "Toozoonin Arabs" were a headlining act, known nationally for their "Daredevil Dervish Tumbling." Our newspaper searches have uncovered no further reference to "Harrison de Buttervitte," whose "black and tan" performance suggests that he was either black or performed in black-face.

MORE THAN 12,000 ATTEND OPENING OF THE ELECTRIC THEATER
Springfield's Newest Place of Amusement Crowded Throughout Day— Long Lines Formed Before Ticket Office

More than 12,000 persons paid admission Sunday afternoon and evening to the handsome Electric Theater that was formally thrown open to amusement lovers of Springfield. Henry Grubel of the Grubel Brothers company, owners of the $75,000 theater, said the opening was the most successful ever held at any of the theaters controlled by the company. Miss Theda Bara, the renowned emotional film actress, appeared at the very height of her success in "Her Double Life," the opening photo-play feature and the Toozoonin Arabs, decidedly the most wonderful aggregation of acrobats that ever appeared in Springfield on a vaudeville bill, responded to no less than half a dozen encores at each performance.

At 12:30 o'clock Sunday, one hour before the time advertised for the opening of the ticket office, a veritable mob thronged the northeast corner of the public square. Each afternoon performance witnessed a packed house and Sunday evening hundreds of visitors were turned from the doors of the show house. At 7:30 o'clock Sunday evening the line waiting for tickets extended west beyond the Nathan Clothing store at Boonville and the public square. Manager William Beckley said that had Springfield not been in the grip of a street car strike it would have been an impossibility to handle the crowds. Despite the fact that no cars were running from the north side hundreds who were eager to witness the spectacular opening of the Electric walked....

Although much publicity had been made regarding the splendor of the new amusement resort the visitors at the opening were astounded at the gorgeousness of the place. The theater was complete and was finished elaborately just in time for the event Sunday.

A feature which attracted unusual interest from the women was the [mezzanine lobby and foyer leading] to the balcony. Here was a beautiful place with every accessory the feminine heart could desire. Finely upholstered chairs and couches offer a place for rest and the decorations are superb. There is an aquarium of spritely goldfish and cages of twittering canaries.

The music, under the direction of Prof. Will Keet, also was a feature that met with instant favor. Prof. Keet and his organization were forced to answer numerous encores.

Today and tomorrow the Electric will present dainty Anita Stewart in the thrilling Vitagraph drama, "The Combat." The vaudeville bill includes Harrison de Buttervitte in black and tan features. The management received so many requests for the reappearance of the Toozoonin Arabs that the "whirlwinds of the desert" will be on stage again today and tomorrow.

Figures and Photo Credits

Figure. Decorative elements. Photographs courtesy of Mark Shipley Photography.

1. October 11, 1926: The Opening
Figure. "A Beautiful Theatre for Springfield." Newspaper advertisement. October 10, 1926. *Springfield Republican.*
Figure. "Wonderland Gillioz." Newspaper article. October 10, 1926. *Springfield Leader.*
Figure. "Come if You Have to Fly." Newspaper advertisement. October 10, 1926. *Springfield Leader.*
Figure. Gillioz on Opening Night. 1926. Photograph courtesy of Special Collections and Archives, Missouri State University.
Figure. Gillioz Marquee and Facade. 1926. Photograph courtesy of Special Collections and Archives, Missouri State University.
Figure. Gillioz Entrance Bay. 1926. Photograph courtesy of Special Collections and Archives, Missouri State University.
Figure. Gillioz Outer Lobby. 1926. Photograph courtesy of Special Collections and Archives, Missouri State University.
Figures. Gillioz Mezzanine Rotunda. 1926. Photographs courtesy of Special Collections and Archives, Missouri State University.
Figure. Gillioz Orchestra Foyer. 1926. Photograph courtesy of Special Collections and Archives, Missouri State University.
Figure. Gillioz Stage.1926. Photograph courtesy of Special Collections and Archives, Missouri State University.
Figure. Gillioz East Arcade. 1926. Photograph courtesy of Special Collections and Archives, Missouri State University.
Figure. Gillioz Balcony. 1926. Photograph courtesy of Special Collections and Archives, Missouri State University.
Figure. Gable Telegram. March 6, 1934. Photograph courtesy of Special Collections and Archives, Missouri State University.

2. Gillioz: The Man and His "Theatre Beautiful"
Figure. "Local Company Plans Theater." Newspaper article. December 7, 1924. *Springfield Leader.*
Figure. M. E. Gillioz. 1926. Photograph courtesy of Special Collections and Archives, Missouri State University.
Figure. Gillioz Theatre in Monett. 1931. Photograph courtesy of Special Collections and Archives, Missouri State University.
Figure. "All Around the Town." Newspaper advertisement. February 1, 1929. *Springfield Daily News.*
Figure. The Landers Theatre. Postcard. Circa 1915. Photograph courtesy of The History Museum for Springfield-Greene County.
Figure. The Jefferson Theatre. 1916. Photograph courtesy of The History Museum for Springfield-Greene County.
Figure. The Electric Theatre. Circa 1939. Photograph courtesy of The History Museum for Springfield-Greene County.
Figure. The Baldwin Theatre. Postcard. Circa 1900. Photograph courtesy of The History Museum for Springfield-Greene County.
Figure. The Springfield Shrine Mosque. Postcard. Circa 1926. Photograph courtesy of The History Museum for Springfield-Greene County.

3. Springfield, The Roaring Twenties, and the Technologies of Leisure
Figure. Cars on the Public Square. Circa 1927. Photograph courtesy of The History Museum for Springfield-Greene County.
Figure. Gillioz on Route 66. Circa 1927. Photograph courtesy of The History Museum for Springfield-Greene County.
Figure. Kilties on Parade. Circa 1926. Photograph courtesy of The History Museum for Springfield-Greene County.
Figure. "The Ozarks Are Calling You." Sheet music. 1926. Photograph courtesy of the Springfield-Greene County Library.
Figure. "Just Ask Springfield Mo." Promotional booklet. Circa 1925. Photograph courtesy of Wayne Glenn.

4. Vaudeville!
Figure. White City Park. Circa 1915. Photograph courtesy of The History Museum for Springfield-Greene County.
Figure. Amateur Orchestra on the Gillioz Stage. Circa 1930. Photograph courtesy of The History Museum for Springfield-Greene County.
Figure. Joe Jackson. Newspaper advertisement. February 18, 1927. *Springfield Daily News.*
Figure. Buster Keaton. Newspaper advertisement. February 20, 1927. *Springfield Daily News.*
Figure. The Circus! Newspaper advertisement. July 31, 1927. *Springfield Leader.*
Figure. *Ankles Preferred.* Newspaper advertisement. June 26, 1927. *Springfield Daily News.*
Figure. "Meet 'Miss Springfield.'" Newspaper advertisement. July 17, 1927. *Springfield Daily News.*
Figure. "Pageant of Glorious Girlhood." Newspaper advertisement. May 26, 1931. *Springfield Press.*
Figure. "Who Will Be Miss Springfield?" 1931. Photograph courtesy Special Collections and Archives, Missouri State University.
Figure. Clinton at the Wurlitzer. Circa 1946. Photograph courtesy of Marilyn Bockharst.
Figure. *La Zingara.* Circa 1940s. Photograph courtesy of Albert Ralls.
Figure. Bob Barker at the Gillioz. Circa 1955. Photograph courtesy of The History Museum for Springfield-Greene County.

5. Lights, Camera,...
Figure. *Lights of New York.* Newspaper advertisement. November 11, 1928. *Springfield News and Leader.*
Figure. Mozark on the Square. Circa 1939. Photograph courtesy of The History Museum for Springfield-Greene County.
Figure. *The Broadway Melody.* Newspaper advertisement. April 12, 1929. *Springfield Leader.*
Figure. Weaver Brothers and Elviry. Circa 1934. Photograph courtesy of Wayne Glenn.
Figure. *Swing Your Lady.* Newspaper advertisement. January 14, 1938. *Springfield Leader and Press.*
Figure. Weavers Arrive at the Gillioz. January 15, 1938. *Springfield Leader and Press.*
Figure. *Jesse James.* Newspaper advertisement. February 2, 1939. *Springfield Leader and Press.*
Figure. Tyrone Power. Autographed portrait. 1938. Photograph courtesy of Special Collections and Archives, Missouri State University.
Figure. *The Shepherd of the Hills.* Newspaper advertisement. July 4, 1941. *Springfield Leader and Press.*
Figure. Parade for *This Is The Army.* 1941. Photograph courtesy of Photograph courtesy of Special Collections and Archives, Missouri State University.
Figure. Box Office for *This Is The Army.* 1941. Photograph courtesy of Special Collections and Archives, Missouri State University.
Figure. *The Robe.* Newspaper advertisement. November 5, 1953. *Springfield News and Leader.*
Figure. *House of Wax.* Newspaper advertisement. May 14, 1953. *Springfield Leader and Press.*
Figure. A Gathering of Gillioz Logos. Photographs courtesy of Craig A. Meyer.

Works Cited

Baldassare, Mark. "Suburban Communities." *Annual Review of Sociology* 18 (1992): 475-494.

Baughman, James L. *The Republic of Mass Culture: Journalism, Filmmaking, and Broadcasting in America Since 1941.* Baltimore: John Hopkins UP, 1992.

Carrara, John. *Enemies of Youth.* 2nd ed. Grand Rapids: Zondervan, 1939.

Chudleigh, Gerry. The Harold Bell Wright Web Site. 1 June 2006. <http://www.hbw.addr.com/index.htm>.

Dark, Harris and Dark, Phyllis. *Springfield of the Ozarks: An Illustrated History.* Woodland Hills, CA: Windsor, 1981.

Ebner, Michael H. "Re-Reading Suburban America: Urban Population Deconcentration, 1810-1980." *American Quarterly* 37 (1985): 368-381.

Erickson, Hal. Plot Synopsis, *This Is The Army. Allmovie.com.* 01 June 2006. <http://allmovie.com/cg/avg.dll>.

———. Plot Synopsis, *She's Working Her Way Through College. Allmovie.com.* 01 June 2006. <http://allmovie.com/cg/avg.dll>.

———. Plot Synopsis, *The Winning Team. Allmovie.com.* 01 June 2006. <http://allmovie.com/cg/avg.dll>.

Gilbert, Wil. Plot Summary, *The Male Animal.* Imb.com. 01 June 2006. <http://www.imdb.com/title/tt0035020/plotsummary>.

Glenn, Wayne. *The Ozarks' Greatest Hits: A Photo History of Music in the Ozarks.* Cassville: Litho Printers, 2005.

Guest, Avery M. "Patterns of Suburban Population Growth, 1970-75." *Demography* 16 (1979): 401-415.

Hocklander, Sony. "Arts, Downtown Enjoy Symbiotic Boom." *Springfield News-Leader.* 10 Mar. 2003: A5.

———. "Backers Never Gave Up on Grand Old Dame." *Springfield News-Leader.* 29 Feb. 2004: L17.

———. "Gillioz Furniture Decorated Property Room." *Springfield News-Leader.* 26 Dec. 2003: B1.

Holsen, James N. *Economic Survey of Missouri.* Saint Louis: Southwestern Bell Telephone Company, 1927.

Ketchum, Richard M. *Will Rogers: His Life and Times.* New York: American Heritage Publishing, 1973.

Keyes, Robert. "Downtown's Renewal Delights Fans of Area." *Springfield News-Leader.* 13 May 2002: A1+.

Lynd, Robert S. and Lynd, Helen Merrell. *Middletown: A Study of American Culture.* New York: Harcourt, 1929.

Marymount, Mark. "Jewell Took Long Path to Jubilee." *Springfield News-Leader.* June 1, 1988. D2+.

McCann, Gerald E. Jr. "The Gillioz Will Rise Again." *Springfield! Magazine.* April 1994: 26.

McLean, Albert F. *American Vaudeville as Ritual.* Lexington: U of Kentucky P, 1965.

Moser, Arthur Paul. "Earliest Motion Pictures Houses in Springfield Came and Went with Rapidity During 1920s." *Springfield! Magazine.* June 1983: 34-35.

———. "Springfield's First Picture Theater Mixed Movies with Four Acts of Vaudeville." *Springfield! Magazine.* May 1983: 38+.

O'Brien, Mike. "Local Lucky Fans Got an Early Glimpse of Elvis." *Springfield News-Leader.* 14 May 2006: C1+.

"Oil Tankers." *Modern Marvels.* History Channel, Springfield, MO. 06 May 2006.

Rafferty, Milton D. *The Ozarks: Land and Life.* Fayetteville: U of Arkansas P, 2001.

Rainey, Tracey. *A Study of the Gillioz Theatre: Its Architecture, History, and the Present Renovation.* M. A. Thesis. Southwest Missouri State University, 2001.

Slide, Anthony, ed. *Selected Vaudeville Criticism.* Metuchen NJ: Scarecrow, 1988.

Spears-Stewart, Reta. *Remembering the Ozark Jubilee.* Springfield: Stewart, Dillbeck and White, 1993.

———. "Weaver Brothers and Elviry." *Springfield! Magazine.* Part 2, Feb. 1989: 61+. Part 5, May 1989: 34+.

Stein, Charles W., ed. *American Vaudeville as Seen by its Contemporaries.* New York: Knopf, 1984.

Tatum, Bil. "'La Traviata' Praised as a Class Act for Springfield." *Springfield News-Leader.* 20 July 1980: B8.

Wagner, Ann. *Adversaries of the Dance: From the Puritans to the Present.* Urbana: U of Illinois P, 1997.

Walker, Don. "Truman and Reagan—'The Winning Team.'" n.p. n.d. 22-24. Truman vertical file, Tthe History Museum for Springfield-Greene County.

Index

94

The design process for this book was assisted
by Maria Gerasimchuk and Colin Wright,
students from the Art and Design Department
of Missouri State University

Cover illustration by Kory Bingaman

Photographs prepared for publication by Kory Bingaman

Photographs of the restoration process by Mark Shipley

Text type set in Chaparral and Isadora by Eric Pervukhin

Layout produced using Adobe InDesign and Adobe Photoshop

Printed and bound by Print Group Inc., Ozark, Missouri

This book was printed in a first edition of 2,500 copies.